Tia's creative use of both sweet and savory pairings, articulate recipes, and precise advice on how to pick great cheeses make for scintillating reading. The magnificent photography is simply wonderful eye candy. *The Art of the Cheese Plate* is truly one of a kind, a spectacular new tome about my favorite food: Cheese.

—JONATHAN WAXMAN, chef, Barbuto, Adele's, and Waxman's

Finally, Tia Keenan gives us the book on how to put together sensuous, delicious, and refreshingly modern cheese plates—all with a good dose of humor and, blessedly, easy-to-follow recipes. Cheese should be, and can be, an everyday food, not just a special-occasion one. *The Art of the Cheese Plate* is everyone's roadmap for serving and eating cheese with inspired style.

—LIZ THORPE, cheese expert and author, *The Book of Cheese*

There aren't many people who know more about cheese than Tia Keenan, which is precisely why it's so impressive that she's managed turn that knowledge into a book that's as accessible as it is whip-smart. At its core, this is a book about flavor and its building blocks. And for that alone it's an essential read for any home cook, drinker, or civilian with a passing interest in what tastes good and why.

—TALIA BAIOCCHI, editor-in-chief of *PUNCH* and author, *Spritz*

I collect cheese books and this is one of the best. Tia Keenan has created a treasure-chest toolbox for food lovers eager to explore the world of cheese. Her cheese knowledge is top-notch and her accompaniments are best in class, making *The Art of the Cheese Plate* a beautiful, intuitive guide to elevating your cheese experience.

—ADAM MOSKOWITZ, founder of The Cheesemonger Invitational

The Art of the Cheese Plate is a remarkable achievement, as practical as it is beautiful. Experienced cheese lovers will find inspiration in Tia's novel pairings and bold accompaniments, while novices will benefit from expert advice on sourcing and serving. This exciting book will change the way you think about cheese.

—MARCUS GLOCKER, chef, Bâtard Tribeca

Cheese lovers with a passion for flavor, cooking, and entertaining have found their ultimate resource. Keenan is a captivating writer with an innate ability to bring together fantasy and practicality. Follow one of her recipes and you'll soon be entertaining without realizing how much fun you're having—and how deliciously simple it is.

—THALASSA SKINNER, co-founder of *Culture: The Word on Cheese*

THE ART OF THE
CHEESE PLATE

PAIRINGS, RECIPES,
STYLE, ATTITUDE

TIA KEENAN

THE ART OF THE
CHEESE PLATE

PHOTOGRAPHS BY
NOAH FECKS

RIZZOLI
NEW YORK

New York · Paris · London · Milan

TO MY PERFECT PAIRING,
HRISTO ZISOVSKI

First published in the United States of America in 2016
by Rizzoli International Publications, Inc.
300 Park Avenue South
New York, NY 10010
www.rizzoliusa.com

© 2016 by Tia Keenan
tiakeenan.com

Photographs © Noah Fecks
noahfecks.com

Food styling by Tia Keenan
Prop styling by Ben Knox and Christopher Spaulding, Reclaim Design
reclaimdesignnyc.com

Design by Lynne Yeamans / Lync

2016 2017 2018 2019 / 10 9 8 7 6 5 4 3 2 1

Distributed in the U.S. trade by Random House, New York
Printed in China

ISBN-13: 978-0-8478-4982-6
Library of Congress Catalog Control Number: 2016932295

THE ART OF THE CHEESE PLATE

INTRODUCTION
7

CHEESE PLATES AND RECIPES
18

INDEX OF CHEESES
184

SOURCES
187

ACKNOWLEDGMENTS
192

THE ART OF THE CHEESE PLATE

There are plenty of books offering in-depth information on all things cheese, from cheese 101 to production and history. Every cheese lover should have at least one of these teaching books in their library. This is not that book. This is a *doing* book, quite specifically about creating artful cheese experiences, with 37 distinct plates comprised of 100 cheeses, 111 pairings, and 84 recipes for impactful accompaniments, with tasting notes and beverage pairings. There are fun plates with familiar cheeses, funky plates with far-out cheeses, and plenty of in-between plates featuring a broad range of milk types, cheese styles, and countries of origin, meant for all kinds of occasions.

Cheese is a nutritional powerhouse—practically a perfect food—a triumph of human craft, born of the necessity to preserve the perishable. And yet what has given cheese longevity as an almost fetishized object is its artistry. Delicious, beautiful, mutable: famously, cheese is "milk's leap toward immortality," but it's also craft's leap toward art. It also occupies a space in our lives between grocery and luxury, and that's why it satiates our hunger, both physical and existential. It can be a humble snack or feast of fantasy. It can be both at the same time. The fact is, most people really, *really* like cheese. Some even claim a cheese "addiction." Even after a decade of composing and serving thousands of cheese plates, I'm continually amazed and surprised by the intense passion cheese lovers have for this ancient agricultural product.

With so much cheese love in the ether, making amazing cheese plates and creating amazing cheese experiences, dare I say cheese *fantasies*, shouldn't be hard. After all, before a cheese plate even hits the table, anticipatory enthusiasm is so high only gross negligence could make for a *bad* cheese experience. Seriously, you'd really have to *try* to ruin a cheese plate.

The thing about great cheese plates is that they inspire us. They're beautiful, delicious, and exciting. Communal boards can be fun (there are even some in this book), but we've all had our regrets when it comes to pillaging a party platter, haven't we? Single-serving plates of artfully paired compositions set a tone of deliberate, exploratory enjoyment. They're like a Saturday night "going out" outfit—a sure sign you're looking for a good time.

The most direct route through these pages is to choose a flight, procure the cheeses and accompaniments, and cook the recipes. This will yield an artful cheese plate, as the title of the book suggests. Perhaps you'll gain a broader perspective on the possibilities and potential of the genre. But my fervent hope is that you'll experience the grace of diving into a creative, cheese-fueled fantasy, and be inspired to explore less direct paths to an amazing cheese plate, like choosing pairings from different plates and combining them to create a new flight, or selecting different cheeses from those found here and pairing them with recommended accompaniments or accompaniments from another plate. Or make your own accompaniments with your own recipes.

Believe it or not, all the cheese plates in this book are easy to make, in most cases requiring little more than forethought and light cooking. Most plates are built around three cheeses, with one purchased and two homemade accompaniments. Including bought or very simply prepared accompaniments saves time and takes full advantage of the many high-quality specialty foods available. Some plates include only one or two cheeses when the cheese or occasion is best suited to a slightly altered format. High-impact, minimal-effort plates of fabulousness are the Holy Grail of entertaining.

Composed cheese plates are also economical, requiring less cheese per person than a traditional communal board (generally one ounce of cheese per guest) with little to no waste (see Figure 4). When paired with unique accompaniments, you get way more bounce to the ounce. Place an amazing cheese plate in front of your guests and you're giving them a bespoke, one-of-a-kind gift.

Almost all of the recipes in this book are quick and relatively simple. They're *accompaniments*, after all—little prepared tidbits meant to enhance your experience of the main attraction: the cheese. In general, the recipes are scaled to accompaniment-appropriate portions meant to serve four. Recipes with built-in leftovers have suggestions for additional uses.

Some of the entries include beverage pairings, suggestions to enhance your experience of the plate, turn you on to some cool juice, and whet your appetite (so you can keep eating more cheese). They're not orthodoxy: The right beverage pairing is the one you feel like drinking. If you're not sure what you feel like drinking, try the suggested pairings.

Bread isn't always necessary when serving composed cheese plates. The accompaniments add substantiality and texture, bread's traditional role on a cheese plate. If you *must* serve bread—because it's expected or you just really like it—keep it simple: a beautifully baked, crisp baguette or a snappy neutral cracker, one selection, maybe two, no need for more than that.

LIFE IS TOO SHORT TO EAT MEDIOCRE CHEESE

You can't make an amazing cheese plate without amazing cheese. Subpar cheese paired with an incredible artisanal jam made from pristine heirloom fruit is still *subpar cheese*. Only the good stuff will do. The cheeses featured in this book are all specialty, artisanal, or farmstead cheeses. They're made with integrity (specialty), very often by hand (artisanal), and sometimes on a farm that produces both the milk and the cheese (farmstead), denoting a baseline of quality across cheese plates.

FIGURE 1:
TYPES OF CHEESE

FRESH
Young, rindless, and so moist they're almost wet, these cheeses are highly perishable and meant to be eaten within days or weeks. Characteristically light, milky, and tangy (see **Fresh & Fundamental**, page 20).

SURFACE RIPENED
Primarily youthful cheeses that run the gamut in terms of flavor, but texturally are characteristically creamy, spreadable, or scoopable, with white "bloomy" rinds of *Penicillium* mold (see **Camembarely**, page 80), blue and gray "ashed" rinds (see **Ashes to Ashes**, page 72), wrinkly rinds of *Geotrichum* mold (see **Bijou**, page 36 and **Chabichou**, page 65), and orange-hued washed rinds of *B. linens* bacteria (see **Stankonia**, page 156).

PASTA FILATA
Made by stretching hot curd (think hand-pulled noodles, but cheese). Includes fresh, milky cheeses (see **Burrata Wishes, Caviar Dreams**, page 180) and aged, firm cheeses like provolone.

SEMI-FIRM/FIRM/HARD
A huge catchall category including several technical styles. These are slicing and grating cheeses, often with natural or waxed rinds (see **Gouda-esque**, page 126, **Pecorino Preservation Society**, page 160, and **Hard Day's Night**, page 148).

BLUE
Simply put: cheeses with blue mold. From moist, creamy, and fruity cheeses (see **Roquefort**, page 29) to dry, firm, earthy cheeses (see **Cayuga Blue**, page 179).

Both the European Union and individual countries within Europe legally regulate the production, quality, and authenticity of their cheeses. **Parmigiano Reggiano** (see page 29) is only "Parmigiano Reggiano" because it's made to a specific set of criteria including (but not limited to) milk type, geography, and production method. There are often dozens (and sometimes even hundreds) of producers of a protected European cheese. Specific producers are named here only when the quality of their brand is particularly distinctive.

On the other hand, it would be unthinkable to *not* name the producer of an American cheese. Unlike in Europe, almost all high-quality cheeses produced in the United States are unique to their producer, with no legal regulation of their provenance and production. *Who* produces the cheese is central to its identity and quality.

The short cheese descriptions employed throughout the book are compromises between technical and practical, consumer-friendly terms. They will help you when buying cheese and describing those cheeses to your guests. Since the cheeses pictured are already cut into individual one-ounce portions, I also describe the paste and rind, so you'll have an idea of what larger cuts of the cheese may look like in a cheese case.

The foundational flavors of cheese (see Figure 2) are a culmination of the breed, diet, and geography of the animal, as well as cheese-making techniques and maturation method. Even with so many moving parts, there are foundational flavors across styles, characteristics that speak to the fingerprint of the milk and the effect of the process on flavor and texture.

The tasting notes and recipes throughout the book reference the base flavors and textures listed, often indicated by the use of a slash. This format is employed in two ways throughout the text: to indicate a combination of base flavors (i.e., milky/ floral) or textures (creamy/moist), and to list more specific iterations of a base flavor (i.e., earthy/mushroom-y) or texture (creamy/curdy). More specific, pinpointed flavors and textures are listed directly underneath the cheese in the short descriptions or in the body of the tasting notes. This format gives you general descriptors (helpful when buying cheese) and a more specific language of flavors (helpful when pairing cheese). An example:

SWEET GRASS DAIRY GREEN HILL

Notes of buttered popcorn and button mushroom, with a creamy paste and white, bloomy rind

Sweet Grass Dairy's award-winning Green Hill captures the essence of Georgia sunshine, with a golden yellow paste of grassy goodness. An earthy/mushroom-y rind encapsulates this crowd-pleasing puck—a mild, creamy cheese with balanced saltiness and a buoyant paste.

Figure 2:
FOUNDATIONAL FLAVORS

MILKY
milk, cream, butter (see **Bianca**, page 23, **Kunik**, page 32, and **Burrata**, page 182)

FLORAL/HERBAL
grass, hay, flowers, herbs (see **Green Hill**, page 82, **Chabichou**, page 65, and **Brebirousse D'Argental**, page 50)

TANGY
citrus, yogurt, crème fraîche (see **Fresh Crottin**, page 36, **Humboldt Fog**, page 75, and **Leonora**, page 115)

EARTHY
mushrooms, soil, fresh vegetables (see **Camembert**, pages 82 to 83, **Clothbound Cheddars**, pages 137 to 138, and **Mahon**, page 116)

TOASTY
nuts, caramelized sugar (see **Manchego**, page 116, **Gruyère**, page 102, and **Grana Padano Riserva**, page 150)

FUNKY
barnyard, charcoal, fermented vegetables (see **Pecorino**, pages 162 to 163, **Époisses**, page 45, and **Limburger**, page 159)

BLUE UMAMI
metals, mold, umami (see **Monte Enebro**, page 75, **Cayuga Blue**, page 179, and **Roquefort**, page 29)

Figure 3:
FOUNDATIONAL TEXTURES

MOIST/CURDY/CHALKY
fresh cheeses and some blue cheeses (see **Fresh & Fundamental**, page 20, and **Roquefort**, page 29)

CREAMY
soft-ripened and some washed and blue cheeses (see **Brie**, pages 28 and 54, **Winnimere**, page 174, and **Gorgonzola Cremificato**, page 61)

PLIABLE/SILKY
Mozzarella, some washed cheeses (see **Mozzarella di Bufala**, page 168, and **Grayson**, page 107)

SEMI-FIRM
younger, aged cheeses and some washed cheeses (see **Quadrello di Bufala**, page 70, and **Young Gouda**, page 110)

FIRM
aged cheeses and some washed cheeses (see **Saint Nectaire**, page 41, and **Barely Buzzed**, page 154)

HARD/CRUMBLY
very aged cheeses (see **Parmigiano Reggiano**, page 29, and **Mimolette**, page 150)

Much like wine, the aroma of cheese can play a role in its flavor, but it can be misleading. In some cases the pungency of a cheese is a fair warning of intense flavor. In others, it's simply more aggressive or concentrated, adding to the sensory experience of the cheese but not always reliable as an indicator of flavor. The surest way to determine the intensity of a cheese is to taste it.

On the other hand, a cheese's *texture* has a profound impact on its flavor, and should be given equal consideration (see Figure 3). The super-funk of a soft cheese like **Limburger** (see page 00) would be intolerable if its texture were hard and waxy like **Mimolette** (see page 00)—it's the texture of the butterfat that makes Limburger's pungency palatable. Similarly, **Mimolette** with the mild, soft flavors of **Bianca** (see page 00) would be an inconceivable letdown. Our palate would be utterly confused by a formidable texture without flavors to match, and vice-versa.

THE PERFECT PAIRING IS THE ONE YOU LIKE

The answer to "Does this pairing work?" is "Did you like it?" Pairing is personal, and don't let anyone—or any book—tell you otherwise. The absolute worst that could happen is you eat something less than delicious. No hearts were broken, no governments toppled. In fact, there is no "perfect pairing"; the very concept eliminates the truly personal and experiential nature of eating.

A successful pairing achieves balance between the cheese and the accompaniment. If one is more charismatic or dominant than the other, the pairing feels off. The saddest pairing is one that leaves you wishing you'd eaten the cheese on its own.

A *supportive* pairing like **Ardrahan & Peanut-Tahini Fudge Roll** (see page 158) reinforces flavors and/or textures latent in the cheese. The first time I tasted Ardrahan, I thought "This is like peanut butter . . . but cheese!" A dense, smooth, peanut-y pairing highlights the cheese's nutty creaminess and earthy saltiness, giving a fuller, more vivid experience. This mimicry can apply to both flavors and textures. The logic of pairing **Meadow Creek Dairy Grayson & Deviled Lemon Curd** (see page 107) is born not only of Grayson's egg-y flavor, but also of its *texture*, which is like the silkiest scrambled eggs you've ever had—silky, in fact, like lemon curd.

A *contrasting* pairing may temper or alter latent flavors and/or textures in a cheese. Acidity is a primary vehicle for contrasting flavors in a pairing, as it *opposes* butterfat. In **Plain Young Gouda & Apple Chutney** (see page 110) the apple chutney contrasts the Gouda because it's so much more acidic. And while the apple may play into the sweet notes of the cheese, it's the savory, contrasting spices in the puckering chutney *up against* the mild cheese that ultimately makes the pairing work. Textural juxtaposition is another way to create contrast. **Winnimere & Mosto Cotto-Glazed Bacon** (see pages 174 to 175) relies in part on the tension between sticky bacon and oozing cheese. In fact, some of the most successful pairings are both *supportive* and *contrasting*. The *textures* of the Winnimere pairing are contrasting, but the *flavors* are supportive, echoing the cheese's meaty tones.

Balance between the weight of the cheese and the accompaniment is crucial. "Weight" is about the overall experience, a culmination of the textures and flavors of both elements. A light/mild/fluffy cheese and a dense/robust/hard accompaniment will rarely find balance together, and vice versa. So a bright, mild, moist cheese is paired with a buoyant, moist, vegetal marshmallow in **Valençay & Matcha Marshmallows** (see page 65), and a hard, robust cheese is paired with a richly flavored, crunchy crisp in **L'Amuse Gouda "Pril" & Coffee-Hazelnut Crisps** (page 111).

As mentioned before, acidity is a central player in many recipes. Whether via citrus, vinegar, or wine, acidity is a counterpoint to butterfat. It *cuts through* cheese, invigorating the senses and combatting palate fatigue. It brightens other flavors and makes shy ingredients shine. Candies also appear quite a bit. The wonderful, varied textures of cooked sugar are a winning combination with cheese (the silky pull of caramel and the crystalline crunch of brittle being particular favorites of mine). Caramelized sugar finds a kindred spirit in cheese. During cheese making, sugars in the milk can caramelize, lending nutty/toasted notes that find a perfect partner in caramel or toffee.

When all elements of a cheese and its accompaniment are in harmony, you may find what's often referred to as the "third taste." This is where the magic happens, when two different flavors come together to create a third flavor, distinct from and greater than the sum of its parts. It doesn't taste like the cheese or like the accompaniment. It tastes like the pairing, completely and singularly unique (see **La Tur with Crispy Prosciutto & Dried Cantaloupe**, page 106, and **Red Hawk with Red Onion, Dill, & Vinegar with Pumpernickel Bread Crumbs**, page 159).

ON PLATING & SERVING

Though I'm sure you've heard this before, cheese is best eaten at room temperature; this rest allows the textures and flavors to bloom. If left wrapped and unrefrigerated, tempering a half-pound piece of cheese takes about half an hour. In most cases, the cheese should be cut into portions immediately before serving to ensure that it doesn't dry out, wilt, or sweat.

One of the most commonly asked questions about cheese is "Do I eat the rind?" Unless the rind is covered in wax, it's edible. In the case of surface-ripened cheeses, the rind is considered a vital part of the overall flavor of the cheese and thus should absolutely be eaten. For cheeses with natural rinds, the decision of whether or not to consume the rind is a matter of personal discretion. Don't be afraid: If you don't like it, don't eat it again.

When it comes to the actual plates used, bigger is definitely better. A crowded plate can feel chaotic and make it hard to enjoy the aesthetic beauty of the presentation.

All the cheese plates in this book are plated left to right, top to bottom, or clockwise from mildest to strongest. Sample the pairings in that order; after tasting all the combinations, mix and match. Surprising new pairings inevitably emerge.

Consider the portion and scale of the cheese and accompaniment. A giant mound of an intensely flavored accompaniment next to a one-ounce piece of cheese won't do either component justice. Err on the side of caution. You can always serve additional accompaniments on the side if you think your guests might want more.

Many plates translate quite easily from single serving to communal board: **Eat Your Idols** (see page 26), **All Saints** (see page 38), **Smooth Moves** (see page 104), and **Vice** (see page 152) are particularly adaptable. Simply account for 1 to 2 ounces of cheese per guest and serve the accompaniments alongside, buffet-style. Cheeses can be sliced or guests can cut a slice from larger pieces.

#CHEESEYOUROWNADVENTURE

So you're planning a quiet, cheese-centric night at home with your bestie or an extravagant spread for a special celebration. Either way, you need to score some good cheese. You're empowered and excited, but you've probably stood in front of a cheese counter before, feeling anxious or overwhelmed. Breathe: It can appear to be an arcane world requiring years of study and plenty of cash, but it's easier than you think to get serious about your cheese. The most helpful tool in your toolbox for creating fabulous cheese plates is knowing how to buy cheese. Consider:

Be in an open relationship with a cheesemonger (or two). Listen to what they have to say about what's in the cheese case. There are so many reasons to take this trusting approach, one of the most significant being that cheese is alive, and like all living things is in flux. A trusted cheesemonger knows what's ripe and can guide you to cheeses that fit the profile you're looking for.

Before you head to the cheese counter, have some simple descriptors ready for cheeses you like or cheeses you're looking for. An adjective or two about the texture and flavor are sufficient: "earthy and hard," "creamy and grassy," or " hard and funky." You'd be surprised how many people say, "I like everything!" but after deeper probing add, "But not this, or that . . . or that." The ability to communicate some of the essential traits you enjoy in cheese in succinct, broad terms will make you a favorite customer (which is another great strategy for scoring the good stuff). Start with the foundational flavors and textures (see Figures 2 and 3) and get more specific as you learn.

When possible, taste the cheese before buying, and resist the temptation to buy it all. Any cheese counter cutting cheese to order should be happy to give you a sample (within reason—please don't make a meal of it). Besides tasting a cheese to determine its quality and appeal, this will help your cheesemonger get to know you, which will help you get good stuff. And even though it's tempting to stock up on cheese, especially when there's so many to try, remember that the best place to store cheese is at the cheese shop; so only buy what you plan on eating within a week or two.

Cheese, like all agricultural products, is seasonal. You can't always get what you want: If it's not in season, it's not in season. Being connected to the rhythms of nature is an important aspect of eating well, and seasonal eating means you're enjoying a product at its peak, when the factors that mark it as singular and special are present. Alpine cheeses are best when the cows have grazed on summer grasses (see **The Hills Are Alive**, page 100). Spring's bright cheeses embody the flavors of renewal (see **Spring, Sprung**, page 84). The decadent velvet pudding of winter spoon cheeses is possible only because of the rich, concentrated milk born of winter hay (see **Rush Creek Weekend**, page 118, and **Winnimere Wonderland**, page 172). Looking forward to January so you can eat spoon cheese is a good thing. There are so few things to look forward to in January, anyhow.

Shop at your farmers' markets. They're a great resource for local cheeses and accompaniments, and provide a perfect opportunity to support up-and-coming producers within your community.

And, finally, embrace the basics of pairing so you can move beyond them. In general, rules don't allow for context, personal taste, or nuance, and are often condescending and needlessly constricting. But I have to admit that they're useful, providing a foundation and structure that make exploration and revelation possible. There's no deliverance without standard delivery.

FIGURE 4:
CHEESE CUTS

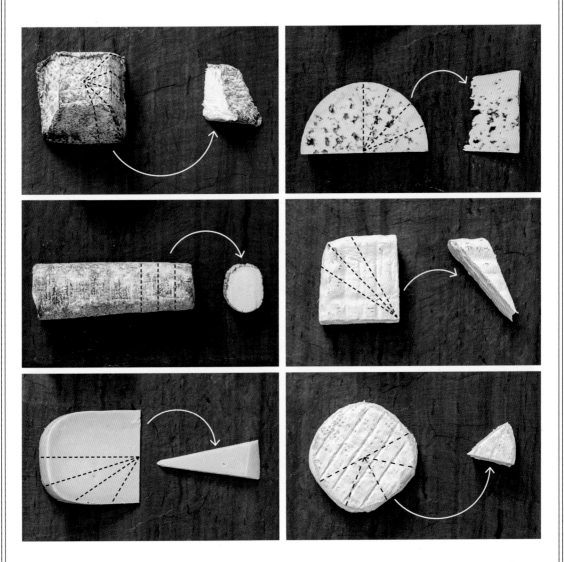

Similar to a pie or cake, the goal when cutting a piece of cheese is to ensure each portion is of similar size and integrity, encompassing a cross-section of the whole, from center to outer rind.

CHEESE PLATES AND RECIPES

Fresh & Fundamental 20
  Sorrel Pesto 23
  Meyer Lemon Marmalade 24
Eat Your Idols 26
  Zucchini Butter 28
  Cranberry-Gin Compote 29
Udder from Another Mother 30
  Carrot Halwa. 32
  Candied Jalapeños 33
Ladies Who Lunch (On Cheese) 34
  Lemon-Chamomile Fudge 36
  Macerated Peaches with
    Orange Blossom & Honey. 37
All Saints 38
  Tequila-Braised Rhubarb 40
  Candied Tomato Pesto 41
Mission: Époissable 42
  Lotus Root & Carrot Chips 45
  Baked Cauliflower Chips. 46
Ewephoric 48
  Roasted Romanesco
    with Tarragon. 50
  Banana-Mango Chutney 51
Berried Treasure 52
  Baked Brie in Kataifi. 54
  Macerated Strawberries with
    Shiso & Black Pepper 55
  Raspberry-Licorice Compote 55
  Pickled Blueberries with
    Ginger & Star Anise 56
Cheese Is for Lovers. 58
  Borschtmallows 60
  Baked Lady Apples with
    Gorgonzola Cremificato
    & Crumbled Amaretti. 61

Joie de Chèvre 62
  Pink Peppercorn Lychee 65
  Matcha Marshmallows. 65
  Tandoori Cashews 66
Buffalo Soldiers. 68
  Sticky Tamarind-Glazed
    Brazil Nuts. 70
  Butternut Squash &
    Golden Raisin Chutney. 71
Ashes to Ashes 72
  Pistachio Pesto &
    Quick-Pickled Cherries. 74
  Celery, Cucumber, &
    Ginger Preserve 75
Belgian Beauts 76
  Charred Scallions with
    Mike's Hot Honey. 78
  Piccalilli 78
  Roasted Concord Grapes
    with Thyme 79
Camembarely 80
  Cracklin' Jack 82
  Creamed Corn &
    Pickled Mustard Seeds. 83
Spring, Sprung. 84
  Roasted Fiddlehead Ferns
    with Sweet Paprika 86
  Butter-Poached Morel
    Mushrooms 87
Wrapture. 88
  Miso-Glazed Carrots. 90
  Grilled Artichokes 91
  Quick-Pickled Seckel Pears. 91
Party Like It's 1979 92
  Port Wine Cheddar 94

Hazelnut-Paprika and
Chive Boursin Cheese Balls 94

Alpine Cheese Fondue 95

Rule, Britannia 96

Quick-Pickled Golden Raisins 98

English Breakfast Tea Jelly 99

The Hills Are Alive 100

Sunflower Seed Brittle 102

Fried Onion Strings............. 103

Smooth Moves 104

Crispy Prosciutto &
Dried Cantaloupe 106

Sparkling Apple Cider Jelly...... 107

Deviled Lemon Curd............ 107

Aging Gracefully................. 108

Apple Chutney 110

Coffee-Hazelnut Crisps 111

Spanish Style 112

Poppy Seed Caviar &
Dragon Fruit Chips........... 115

Sweet Potato Butter & Fried Sage. 116

Rush Creek Weekend 118

Cast-Iron Endives................ 120

Tempura Watercress & Olives 120

Anatomy 101..................... 122

Lavender-Quince Paste........... 124

Black & White Sesame Crisps..... 125

Gouda-esque 126

Date-Glazed Baby Eggplant
with Orange & Fennel 128

Spiced Corn Nut Brittle.......... 129

Portugueezy 130

Doce de Tomate
(Sweet Tomato Jam) 132

Pickled Chinese Sausage
& Celery Slaw................. 132

Port-Glazed Figs with Aniseed.... 133

Love Letter to Clothbound Cheddar .. 134

More Modern Mincemeat........ 137

Cheddar Cheese Straw Brickle.... 138

Sargeant Peppers................. 140

Green Peppercorn Meringue 142

Basil & Preserved Lemon Pesto ... 143

Smoky Bandits.................. 144

Pan-Roasted Plums with
Scotch & Lime 146

Hard Day's Night 148

Gin Negroni.................. 150

Cognac Sidecar 151

Vice 152

Dark Chocolate–Espresso
Ganache 154

Glazed Medjool Dates........... 155

Stankonia 156

Peanut-Tahini Fudge Roll 158

Pumpernickel Bread Crumbs 159

Pecorino Preservation Society 160

Better Wet Walnuts............ 162

Bran Cereal Crackers.......... 163

Flight of Fancy................... 166

Piquillo Pepper Gastrique 168

Dulcey Champagne Ganache 169

Winnimere Wonderland 172

Ritz Cracker–Bacon Brickle 174

Mosto Cotto–Glazed Bacon 175

Kind of Blue 176

White Chocolate, Almond,
& Castelvetrano Olive Bark 178

Sautéed Mushrooms with
Lemon & Thyme 179

Burrata Wishes, Caviar Dreams 180

Purple Potato Chips 182

Lemony Polenta Blini 182

FRESH & FUNDAMENTAL

Fresh cheeses paired with fun, focused accompaniments highlight the intrinsic flavors of cow, sheep, and goat's milk. Bread isn't a necessity with composed cheese plates, but here it's a useful platform for the clean, mild cheeses and custom-fit pairings, which shine when slathered on a hunk of crusty baguette.

**VERMONT CREAMERY
FRESH GOAT CHEESE**
Pasteurized Goat's Milk
Websterville, Vermont

MEYER LEMON MARMALADE

**3-CORNER FIELD
FARM BREBIS
BLANCHE**
Pasteurized Sheep's Milk
Shushan, New York

BEE RAW BUCKWHEAT
HONEY

**HAWTHORNE
VALLEY FARM
BIANCA**
Pasteurized Cow's Milk
Ghent, New York

SORREL PESTO

HAWTHORNE VALLEY FARM BIANCA

Notes of sweet cream and hay

Creamy/moist/tangy: Hawthorne Valley Farm Bianca embodies the classic notes of a fresh cow's milk cheese, with clean, grassy flavors and a smooth paste.

SORREL PESTO

You'll need sorrel, garlic, lemon, Bianca cheese, extra-virgin olive oil

There are three types of culinary sorrel. Use broad-leaf sorrel, which has the sour citrus and grass flavors we're looking for. The young, small leaves are flavorful and tender, while the large leaves are best saved for cooking.

Sorrel pesto reinforces the grassy qualities of Bianca, adding lemony brightness to Bianca's creaminess. We're parsimonious with garlic here: Too much could easily overpower the cheese. A generous dose of lemon highlights the citrus notes of the sorrel as well as Bianca's tang and prevents the fetching bright green sorrel from oxidizing.

Coarsely chop **4 cups tightly packed stemmed sorrel leaves**. In a food processor, combine with **1 garlic clove** and the **zest and juice of 1 lemon** and pulse until thoroughly combined. Add **2 ounces Bianca cheese** and **¼ cup extra-virgin olive oil**. Process for another minute or two, until smooth. Season with salt and pepper.

Makes 1 cup. Store in the refrigerator, its surface covered with a thin layer of olive oil and tightly sealed, for up to 2 weeks. Also a great match with **Haystack Mountain Goat Dairy Camembert** (see page 83). Excellent tossed with pasta, on a sandwich with roast turkey or beef, or as a garnish for vegetable soup.

3-CORNER FIELD FARM BREBIS BLANCHE
Notes of scorched milk, clove, and lemon

Creamy/curdy/funky: Brebis Blanche is a highly seasonal cheese made from the milk of sheep grazing on pasture from April through September. Sheep's milk is exceedingly nutritious, with a high fat content and a plethora of concentrated minerals. Its sweet and barnyard flavors make it worth seeking out, despite its rarity in the United States.

Bee Raw Washington State Buckwheat Honey is an unfiltered, single-varietal dark honey with understated sweetness and clove and molasses flavors that draw out the herbal and caramelized notes of the Brebis Blanche.

VERMONT CREAMERY FRESH GOAT CHEESE
Notes of lemon, limestone, and clover

Creamy/chalky/tangy: Vermont Creamery Fresh Goat Cheese is the benchmark American chèvre. (In France, *chèvre* refers to all cheeses made of goat's milk; in the United States, it typically refers to fresh goat cheese only.) Vermont Creamery Fresh Goat Cheese embodies the essence of what makes chèvre distinctive, with zippy citrus, mineral, and grass tones.

MEYER LEMON MARMALADE
You'll need Meyer lemons, sugar, bay leaf, vanilla bean

The concentrated lemon of the marmalade highlights the citrus notes typical of fresh goat cheeses, while bay leaf adds a subtle herbal note that complements similar undertones in the cheese.

Boil 3 cups water and pour over **12 Meyer lemons** in a colander. Scrub the lemon rinds gently with a vegetable scrubber to remove any wax.

Juice the lemons and set the juice aside. With a sharp paring knife, remove the remaining pulp and slice the peels into thin strips. Place the peels in a large, heavy-bottomed saucepan, cover with 6 cups water, and bring to a boil. Boil for 2 minutes. Drain the peels and rinse with cool water. Repeat this process four more times.

In a large, heavy-bottomed saucepan, combine the lemon juice, peels, **2½ cups sugar**, **1 bay leaf**, and **½ teaspoon kosher salt** and cook over medium heat, stirring occasionally and skimming off the foam once or twice, for 30 minutes. Add **1 split vanilla bean** and **¼ teaspoon kosher salt** and cook for 15 minutes more, or until the marmalade thickens (don't worry if it isn't as thick as you'd anticipated—it will gel more as it cools). Remove from the heat and discard the vanilla bean.

Makes 3 cups. Store in tightly sealed glass jars in the refrigerator for up to 1 month. Also delicious paired with **Bûcheron** (see page 66). Great in marinades and glazes, baked in cookies and pastries, or on Sunday morning buttered biscuits.

The best fresh cheeses are local out of necessity; cheeses closest to home are handled less and are redolent of the local terroir. The fresh cheeses featured in this flight are local to New York City. To find fresh cheeses from your area, visit a nearby farmers' market or cheese shop.

DRINK ME

White wine is the go-to for many cheeses, and almost mandatory with delicate fresh cheeses like the ones in this flight. Sauvignon blanc of any origin offers plenty of high-acid citrus/grass notes with a dry, crisp, refreshing finish. Both "old world" and "new world" sauvignon blancs highlight similar notes in the cheeses.

Domaine Vacheron Sancerre
Sauvignon blanc grapes, Loire Valley, France
Light body with notes of fresh grass and lemon peel.

Craggy Range "Te Muna Road" Sauvignon Blanc
Sauvignon blanc grapes, Martinborough, New Zealand
Light body with notes of lime blossom and stone fruit.

PAPILLON
BLACK LABEL
ROQUEFORT
Raw Sheep's Milk
Midi-Pyrénées, France

CRANBERRY-GIN
COMPOTE

BRIE FERMIER
JOUVENCE
Pasteurized Cow's Milk
Île-de-France, France

ZUCCHINI BUTTER

CRAVERO PARMIGIANO REGGIANO

Raw Cow's Milk
Emilia-Romagna, Italy

LIDDABIT FIG-RICOTTA
CARAMELS

EAT YOUR IDOLS

Head straight for the idols—those cheeses we know and love—and transform them. Be bold. Break free from dried fruit and nuts; revel in a new approach, boldly exploring flavor and texture. A savory vegetable "butter," a cheese-inflected caramel, and a tart, boozy compote are your entry into the exciting world of artful pairing.

BRIE FERMIER JOUVENCE
Notes of béchamel, white pepper, and creamed corn, with a creamy, sticky paste and white bloomy rind

Brie Fermier Jouvence is a smaller-scale French Brie amid a sea of industrial wheels dominating the American market, proof that Brie can be more than a monotonous people-pleaser. Brie Fermier Jouvence has flavor fortitude, with slightly funky wet earth and mushroom notes, like dipping a homemade biscuit into a hearty cream of mushroom soup.

ZUCCHINI BUTTER
You'll need zucchini, olive oil, shallot, lemon, fresh thyme, unsalted butter

A nice hit of lemon brightens this fresh zucchini accompaniment, which underscores the earthy, fungal notes of the Brie's rind. Lemony acidity and the sweetness of the thyme punctuate the cheese's rich paste. Don't stir too much while cooking—you want the zucchini to get a little crusty in the pan, as caramelization releases its sweetness.

Coarsely grate **1 pound zucchini**, place in a colander in the sink, and toss with **½ teaspoon kosher salt**. Drain for 10 minutes, press out any excess water, and set aside on a clean paper towel.

Heat **2 tablespoons olive oil** in a medium sauté pan over medium heat. Cook **1 diced shallot** until fragrant, 2 to 3 minutes. Toss in the zucchini, the **zest of 1 lemon**, and **2 sprigs fresh thyme**. Raise the heat to medium-high and sauté, stirring occasionally, for 10 minutes. Add the **juice of 1 lemon** and stir to deglaze the pan, then make a well in the center, add **1 tablespoon butter**, and reduce the heat to low. As the butter melts, gently swirl it into the zucchini. Cook for 5 minutes more, or until the zucchini is very soft. Season with salt and pepper. Serve at room temperature.

Makes 1 cup. Store in an airtight container in the refrigerator for up to 2 days. Also yummy with **Selles-sur-Cher** (see page 74) or **Caerphilly** (see page 98). Great on a tomato sandwich with a couple of slices of **Barilotto** (see page 70).

CRAVERO PARMIGIANO REGGIANO
Notes of butterscotch, eucalyptus, and sweet vermouth, with a hard, crumbly paste

Parmigiano Reggiano isn't just for grating, and can be a great choice for a cheese plate, especially when it's an expertly matured, high-quality Parm. Cravero Parmigiano Reggiano is typically aged for 24 months, with complex, sweet, herbal/grassy flavors that are often absent in more ho-hum specimens of the "King of Cheese."

Liddabit Fig-Ricotta Caramels are made with **Salvatore Bklyn Smoked Whole Milk Ricotta** (see page 146), balsamic vinegar reduction, and figs. The sweet, milky, earthy notes of the caramels draw out the subtle fresh hay/barnyard flavors of the Parmigiano Reggiano. Plus, everyone loves candy. Tasty paired with **Cabra Raino** (see page 132).

PAPILLON BLACK LABEL ROQUEFORT
Notes of buttermilk and plum wine, with a creamy, slightly gritty paste

Roquefort is aged in the enormous natural caves of Combalou Mountain in south-central France. One of the most iconic blue cheeses around, it's renowned for its rich, silky, craggy texture and funky, dark fruit flavors.

CRANBERRY-GIN COMPOTE
You'll need lime, unsalted butter, bay leaf, cranberries, sugar, gin, allspice berries

Contrast is the name of the game here. Creamy, salty Roquefort is lashed by the pucker-your-lips, sweet-and-tart trifecta of cranberry, gin, and lime. I chose frozen cranberries for this compote, as they're available year-round.

Peel ¼ **lime** in large strips with a vegetable peeler, avoiding the pith.

In a medium saucepan, melt **1 tablespoon butter** over medium heat until foaming. Add **1 bay leaf** and the lime peel and cook for a minute or two. Add **8 ounces thawed frozen cranberries**, **¼ cup sugar**, **¼ cup good, flavorful gin** (I used **The Botanist Gin**, which has intense herbaceousness), and a **pinch of salt**. Add **1 tablespoon allspice berries** and cook until bubbling. Reduce the heat to low and simmer for 10 minutes, or until the cranberries burst and the compote thickens. Cool to room temperature, discard the bay leaf, lime peel, and allspice berries, and serve.

Makes 1 cup. Store in an airtight container in the refrigerator for up to 4 days. Also delicious with **Smoked Ricotta** (see page 146).

UDDER FROM ANOTHER MOTHER

There's nothing mixed up here, other than the milk. Amped-up amalgams of cow, goat, and sheep's milk prove the sum is greater than its parts, even in cheese. When desirable traits are cherry-picked by cheese makers, texture and flavor triumph. Cooked accompaniments need a day to settle before serving, making this a great do-ahead plate. Serve to iconoclasts, artists, or chosen family—they'll appreciate the perks of *lactodiversity*.

VALDEON
Pasteurized Cow and Goat's Milk
Castilla y León, Spain

CANDIED JALAPEÑOS

NETTLE MEADOW
FARM KUNIK
Pasteurized Cow and Goat's Milk
Warrensburg, New York

DANG ROASTED COCONUT
CHIPS & WILD HIBISCUS
FLOWER CO. WILD HIBISCUS
FLOWERS IN SYRUP

GABIETOU
Raw Cow and Sheep's Milk
Aquitaine, France

CARROT HALWA

NETTLE MEADOW FARM KUNIK

Notes of cultured butter, toasted flour, and warm hay, with a dense, creamy paste and white bloomy rind

Nettle Meadow Farm Kunik is a decadent triple-crème cheese tucked inside a rind that's as soft, white, and plush as a hotel bathrobe. The bright acidity of goat's milk tempers the richness of Kunik's cow's milk cream.

Dang Roasted Coconut Chips add welcome crunch and mellow coconut creaminess to the pairing. **Wild Hibiscus Flower Co. Wild Hibiscus Flowers in Syrup** are straight-up eye candy and contrast Kunik's rich flavor with a much needed hit of sweet and sour.

GABIETOU

Notes of buttered toast and macadamia nuts with a firm, supple paste and bright orange-hued washed rind

Gabietou is washed in brine made from local warm water springs and rock salt. A sophisticated snacker, something you could eat in excess with guests of varied tastes, Gabietou has plenty of earthy, briny notes and sweet, toasty flavors.

CARROT HALWA

You'll need coconut oil, golden raisins, cardamom pods, carrot, lime, allspice, ginger, sweetened condensed milk

The wet earth of carrot and the tropical notes of coconut oil and lime highlight the fruity/yeasty aspects of the cheese. Note that the halwa needs to chill overnight.

Heat **2 tablespoons coconut oil** in a saucepan over medium heat until shimmering and fragrant. Add **½ cup golden raisins** and cook until just starting to brown, 4 to 5 minutes. Transfer to a small bowl, then add **15 crushed cardamom pods** to the pan and cook until fragrant, 2 to 3 minutes. Transfer to the bowl with the raisins. Add **2 cups shredded carrots** to the saucepan, raise the heat to medium-high, and sauté, stirring frequently, until softened. Return the raisins and cardamom to the pan and add **½ teaspoon ground allspice**, **½ teaspoon ground ginger**, **zest of 1 lime**, and a **pinch of salt**. Stir to combine thoroughly.

Add **1 cup sweetened condensed milk**, reduce the heat, and simmer, stirring frequently, for 15 minutes, or until most of the liquid has evaporated. When the halwa holds its shape when pushed to the side of the pan, it's done.

Press the halwa into a loaf pan, cover with plastic wrap, and refrigerate overnight. Cut into squares and serve slightly chilled or at room temperature.

Makes about 12 squares. Store in the refrigerator wrapped in plastic wrap for up to 3 days. Also keen on **Piper's Pyramid** (page 86). Great with yogurt and nuts for breakfast.

VALDEON
Notes of tobacco, minerals, and seaweed, with a dense, fudge-like paste

Valdeon exemplifies the sophisticated robustness of Spanish cheeses. Dense, fudgy, and creamy, with abundant pockets of granular blue and green mold, it has a peppery, vegetal bite. Subtle pine notes are like a walk in the forest.

CANDIED JALAPEÑOS
You'll need jalapeño peppers, sugar

Think of these as minimalist jalapeño jam: a simple, elegant delivery of sweet, spicy deliciousness that picks up similar notes in the Valdeon. Remove membranes and seeds, and the flavor of jalapeño is quite pleasing: earthy/vegetal, with just a whisper of fire. Note that the peppers need to dry overnight.

Slice **4 fat jalapeños** along one side, but do not cut in half. Keep the stem attached and intact. With a very small spoon or fork, carefully remove the seeds and membranes.

Bring a medium saucepan of water to a boil and blanch the jalapeños for 2 to 3 minutes. Drain.

In a small saucepan, combine **2 cups water** and **1 cup sugar** and cook over medium heat, stirring occasionally, until the sugar has dissolved. Add the jalapeños and cook for 5 minutes, then reduce the heat to low and cook, turning the jalapeños every 30 minutes, for 2 to 2½ hours, until they darken and turn slightly translucent. Cool to room temperature in the syrup.

Set a wire rack over a baking sheet. Set the jalapeños on the rack cut-side down and drain in a cool, dry place for 12 to 24 hours.

Makes 4. Wouldn't kick **Gouda "Signature"** (see page 111) out of bed. Save the jalapeño syrup: It's delicious, mixed with tequila and lime.

DRINK ME
Paul Blanck Riesling
Riesling grapes, Alsace, France
Light-medium body with notes of lemon, pineapple, and wet stone

It'd be a crime not to pair Riesling with *something* in this book, as its bright acidity is typically a winner with a broad range of cheeses. It's a particularly great match with piquant and tropical flavors, which are abundant in this flight.

LEMON-CHAMOMILE FUDGE

VERMONT CREAMERY FRESH CROTTIN
Pasteurized Goat's Milk
Websterville, Vermont

MACERATED PEACHES WITH ORANGE BLOSSOM & BASIL

LADIES WHO LUNCH (ON CHEESE)

A fanciful cheese-centric tea party for a buffet brunch or light lunch, where guests are free to gorge on compact jewels of goat cheeses paired with sweet, floral accompaniments and blooming herbal tea.

SPOONABLE FLOWERY
LAVENDER CARAMEL

VERMONT
CREAMERY BIJOU
Pasteurized Goat's Milk
Websterville, Vermont

VERMONT CREAMERY FRESH CROTTIN
Notes of lemon, limestone, and clover, with a creamy, dense, fresh paste

VERMONT CREAMERY BIJOU
Notes of chamomile, honeycomb, and fresh hay, with a dense, fudgy paste and wrinkled Geotrichum rind

Easy-to-love cheeses are key when serving a limited selection to a large group. Vermont Creamery's Fresh Crottin and Bijou embody the bright, clean flavors of young goat cheeses, with plenty of tangy/grassy/herbal/citrus notes. They're also perfect for a buffet: Finished in three or four bites, they're elegant and approachable, and eaten succinctly.

Fresh Crottin and Bijou both pair well with floral accompaniments, which draw out their herbal/grassy notes. Guests can experiment with combinations, finding the pairings they like best. Spread a slice of baguette with Fresh Crottin with **Macerated Peaches**, or dip Bijou into a luscious pool of **Spoonable Flowery Lavender Caramel**, savoring a sweet, floral, tangy bite—or alternate between both cheeses while nibbling on white chocolate–laced **Lemon-Chamomile Fudge**. Whatever your choice, a proper cup of blooming white tea (which you could serve hot or iced, depending on the season) works its charms: comforting, soothing, and just tannic enough to keep everyone eating.

LEMON-CHAMOMILE FUDGE
You'll need chamomile tea, cream cheese, vanilla bean, lemon, confectioners' sugar, white chocolate

Fudge is most often associated with holidays, vacations, and down-home family gatherings. Flavored with lemon and chamomile and paired with a fine goat cheese, it's transformed into an elegant companion yet retains its warm and fuzzy. The creamy, tangy/citrus/herbal notes of the fudge play into similar notes in Fresh Crottin and Bijou.

Oil a loaf pan and line it with parchment paper so that the paper overhangs the edges of the pan.

Bring **¼ cup water** to a boil in a small saucepan and turn off the heat. Add **3 tablespoons loose-leaf chamomile tea** and steep for 20 minutes. Strain the tea into the bowl of a stand mixer, pressing on the solids to extract as much flavor as possible. Discard the tea leaves.

Add **8 ounces softened cream cheese**, the **seeds from 1 vanilla bean, 1 tablespoon lemon zest**, and **¼ teaspoon kosher salt** to the bowl with the chamomile concentrate. Fit the mixer with the whisk attachment and beat on medium speed until completely smooth. Turn the mixer to low, add **3 cups sifted confectioners' sugar** 1 cup at a time, and mix until thoroughly blended.

In a medium saucepan, melt **1½ pounds white chocolate**. With the mixer running on low speed, slowly drizzle the chocolate into the cream cheese mixture.

Pour the fudge into the prepared pan. Refrigerate for 1 hour, then cover and chill overnight. Lift the fudge from the pan using the overhanging parchment as handles and cut into 1-inch squares. Serve chilled.

Makes about 24 squares. Tightly wrap in plastic wrap and store in the refrigerator for up to 5 days. Also yummy with **Chabichou** (see page 65) and **Bûcheron** (see page 66). Send your guests home with leftovers.

Spoonable Flowery Lavender Caramel pairs especially well with Bijou, whose dense, velvety paste is mirrored by the sumptuous pull of caramel. Lavender accentuates its delicate honey and herbal notes. A little goes a long way when pairing with Fresh Crottin, which is more delicate than Bijou. Wouldn't kick **Barely Buzzed** (see page 154) or **Casatica di Bufala** (see page 61) out of bed.

MACERATED PEACHES WITH ORANGE BLOSSOM & BASIL
You'll need basil, sugar, lemon, orange liqueur such as Grand Marnier or curacao, orange blossom water, peaches

Rinse and dry **1 cup packed basil leaves**. Finely chop in a mini food processor, add **¼ cup sugar**, and pulse until combined. Transfer to a large nonreactive bowl and stir in **2 tablespoons fresh lemon juice**, **1 tablespoon orange liqueur**, and **1 tablespoon orange blossom water**. Fold in **2 pounds sliced pitted ripe peaches**, cover, and refrigerate for 2 to 4 hours. Serve at room temperature.

Makes about 3 cups. Also a great match with **Brebis Blanche** (see page 24) and **Anton's Liebe Blond** (see page 60). Needless to say, delicious spooned over vanilla ice cream.

DRINK ME
Art of Tea "Halo"
White flowering tea
Light body with notes of jasmine, vanilla, and white peach

Tea can pair well with cheese; it's comforting, flavorful, and, like wine, has tannins, which express a bitterness that's soothed by butterfat. Fresh Crottin and Bijou are on the genteel end of the cheese spectrum, so a light, floral flowering tea like Halo is a good choice. It makes a beautiful presentation—like a corsage in a cup.

SAINT-ANDRÉ
Pasteurized Cow's Milk
Coutances, France

TEQUILA-BRAISED RHUBARB

SAINTE-MAURE
DE TOURAINE
Pasteurized Goat's Milk
Sainte-Maure de Touraine, France

FAT TOAD FARM CINNAMON
GOAT'S MILK CARAMEL

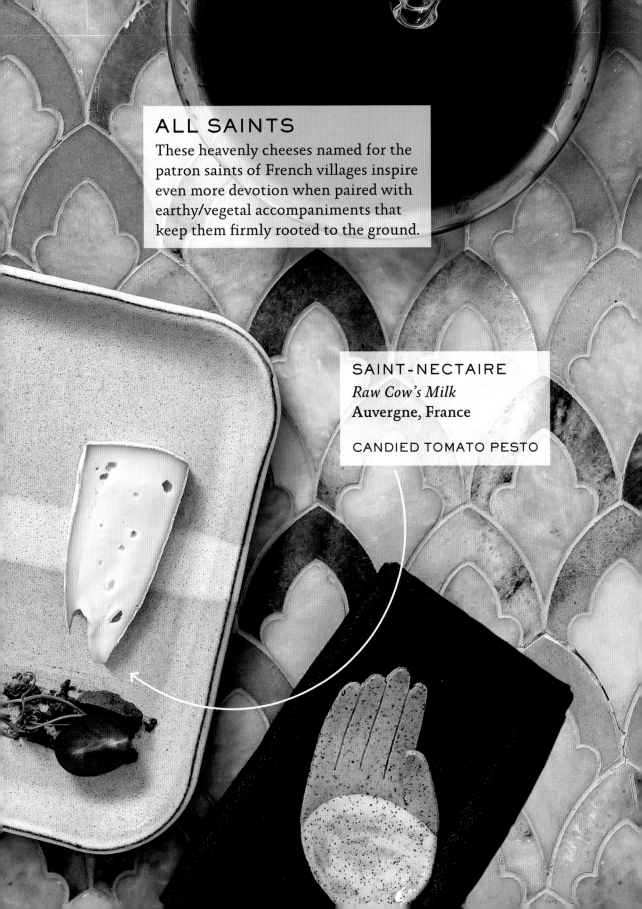

ALL SAINTS

These heavenly cheeses named for the patron saints of French villages inspire even more devotion when paired with earthy/vegetal accompaniments that keep them firmly rooted to the ground.

SAINT-NECTAIRE

Raw Cow's Milk
Auvergne, France

CANDIED TOMATO PESTO

SAINT-ANDRÉ

Notes of heavy cream, talcum powder, and button mushroom, with a rich, creamy paste and white bloomy rind

Saint-André tastes like salted butter with a rind, so what's not to love? It's a pleasing, easy-to-find cheese when you need to compose a cheese plate on the fly, and a godsend for creamy-cheese lovers.

TEQUILA-BRAISED RHUBARB

You'll need rhubarb, lime, tequila, honey, allspice berries, cinnamon stick, vanilla bean

The salinity of the cheese brings a salted-rim-on-a-margarita vibe to this pairing, and the tangy, boozy flavors of rhubarb are an antidote to the triple-crème assault of Saint-André.

Preheat the oven to 400°F. Cut **2 medium stalks rhubarb** into 2-inch pieces. Remove the peel from **half a lime** in thick strips with a vegetable peeler.

Whisk together **¼ cup good tequila** (I use **Don Julio Reposado**), **¼ cup honey**, the **lime peel, 1 tablespoon lime juice, 1 teaspoon allspice berries, 1 cinnamon stick**, the **seeds from 1 vanilla bean**, and a **pinch of kosher salt**. Toss together and transfer to a broiler-safe baking dish. Cover with aluminum foil and bake for 15 minutes, then remove the foil, turn the oven to broil, and broil until the rhubarb has some color, 2 to 3 minutes. The rhubarb should be soft but still hold its shape. Remove and discard the lime peel, allspice berries, and cinnamon stick, and season with pepper. Spoon some of the pan juices over the rhubarb when serving.

Makes enough for 4. Also keen on **Kunik** (see page 32), **Valençay** (see page 65), and **Goat Camembert** (see page 85). Serve leftovers the next morning tsmeared on toast with cream cheese or ricotta.

SAINTE-MAURE DE TOURAINE

Notes of yeast doughnut, barnyard, and creamed honey, with a moist, dense paste and ashed rind

Sainte-Maure de Touraine, a creamy/citrusy log with distinct walnut and wet bark notes, has been crafted in the Loire Valley for more than a thousand years.

The goat's milk tang and cinnamon infusion of **Fat Toad Farm Cinnamon Caramel** is key to this pairing: The earthy/woodsy caramel plays against the tangy/citrus notes of the cheese, buoying its nutty aspects. Also delicious with **Clothbound Cheddars** (see pages 137 to 138) and **Monte Enebro** (see page 75).

SAINT-NECTAIRE
Notes of hazelnut, Grandpa's sweater, and wet earth, with a supple, semi-firm paste and natural rind

Saint-Nectaire is traditionally made from the milk of cows grazing on volcanic pasture, lending distinct charcoal notes to the milk, and is aged on rye-straw mats that impart earthy black truffle tones.

CANDIED TOMATO PESTO
You'll need extra-virgin olive oil, honey, lemon, fresh ginger, sugar, plum tomatoes, parsley, fennel fronds, garlic, red pepper flakes, almonds, panko bread crumbs

Tomatoes are the anchor here; the ginger and honey boost the complexity but hang in the background. Be sparing in this pairing: A touch of pesto plays well with the earthy, charred notes in Saint-Nectaire, but too much obscures its more subtle flavors.

Preheat the oven to 225°F. Line a baking sheet with parchment paper.

In a medium bowl, whisk together **2 tablespoons extra-virgin olive oil**, **2 tablespoons honey**, and the **juice of ½ lemon**. Whisk in **1 teaspoon grated fresh ginger**, **1 tablespoon sugar**, and **2 teaspoons kosher salt**. Quarter **2 pounds ripe plum tomatoes** and toss them with the marinade. Marinate for 20 minutes, then spread the tomatoes over the baking sheet and bake for about 2 hours, until they have lost most of their moisture (the cooking time will vary depending on the ripeness of the tomatoes). Cool on the pan.

Pulse the cooled tomatoes in a food processor, then add **1 cup parsley leaves**, **½ cup fennel fronds**, **1 teaspoon chopped fresh ginger**, **1 chopped garlic clove**, **½ teaspoon red pepper flakes**, **¼ cup chopped raw almonds**, **¼ cup panko bread crumbs**, the **juice of ½ lemon**, and **¼ cup extra-virgin olive oil**. Process until smooth, adding a bit more bread crumbs or olive oil to achieve a thick paste. Taste and adjust the seasoning if needed.

Makes 2 cups. Store in an airtight container in the refrigerator for up to 1 week. Wouldn't kick **Manchego** (see page 116) or **Berkswell** (see page 98) out of bed.

DRINK ME
Domaine Philippe Faury Saint-Joseph Rouge
Syrah grapes, Northern Rhône, France
Medium-full body with notes of rosemary, black pepper, and beef bouillon

In general, white wines are a much better match for a broader range of cheeses than red wine. But sometimes you just want to drink red wine, so they're included in several beverage pairings. The slightly meaty, herbal tones of this stalwart Syrah work best with the Saint-Nectaire and Candied Tomato Pesto pairing.

LOTUS ROOT
CHIPS

CARROT
CHIPS

ÉPOISSES BERTHAUT
Pasteurized Cow's Milk
Burgundy, France

MISSION: ÉPOISSABLE

Sticky, silky, stinky Époisses inspires devotion—it's one of the most coveted spoon cheeses around. "Spoon cheese" isn't a technical term; it's the pet name for cheeses so creamy and pudding-y, spoon trumps knife. Served in its iconic wooden box with a medley of colorful vegetable chips, it's a funky take on chips and dip.

CAULIFLOWER CHIPS

ÉPOISSES BERTHAUT

Notes of bacon fat, almond paste, and carrot peel, with a silky, creamy paste and orange-hued washed rind

The first thing you'll notice about Époisses is its smell—because it stinks. Barnyard, stewed cauliflower, body funk, it's all there. Then there's the color: a striking lacquered autumnal orange. Finally, its intense flavor and mouthfeel, the cream, salt, and fat mingling with animal, vegetable, and mineral tones, all wrapped up in velvety smoothness. Younger pucks are creamy but still maintain their shape; maturer wheels are quite runny.

To soften a too-firm Époisses, or if you simply prefer it warm, first let the cheese come to room temperature and preheat the oven to 250°F. Remove the cheese and line its box with a sheet of parchment paper wide enough to overhang the edges. Return the cheese to its box and bake uncovered on a baking sheet until molten in the center, about 10 minutes. Serve warm. If your Époisses is ripe and already runny, you can forgo this step and serve it at room temperature.

LOTUS ROOT & CARROT CHIPS

You'll need lotus root, carrot, high-heat frying oil such as canola, grapeseed, or peanut oil

Peel **1 medium lotus root** (about 1 pound). Cut crosswise into $1/8$-inch-thick slices with a mandoline or very sharp knife. Soak in cold water for 30 minutes.

In a high-sided heavy-bottomed pot, heat **2 cups oil** over medium heat to 375°F.

Choose **4 big, thick carrots** (about a pound's worth)—the bigger the better. Peel the carrots, but don't trim the tops. With the stem closest to you, slice long ribbons of carrot with a vegetable peeler, rotating the carrot as you peel.

Fry the carrots in four batches. Remove them from the oil when their color just starts to darken and drain on paper towels (the carrots will continue to cook as they drain, and crisp as they cool). Return the oil to 375°F after each batch. You don't need to salt the carrot chips, as the Époisses will provide the salt in this pairing.

Dry the sliced lotus root on paper towels. Fry the lotus root in the hot oil in batches of a dozen or so, until pale golden. Return the oil to 375°F after each batch. Drain the chips on paper towels. Again, there's no need to salt.

Makes 2 cups. Carrot chips should be eaten the same day they're made. Lotus chips can be made 1 day in advance and stored in an airtight, paper towel–lined container.

BAKED CAULIFLOWER CHIPS
You'll need cauliflower, olive oil, white pepper

The vegetal/funky flavors in cauliflower can be awesome with cheese, as long as they're handled capably. Caramelization is crucial, adding sweetness and texture while subduing the somewhat sulfurous quality of the veg. Limp *Brassica* flavors and aromas (think boiled cabbage or broccoli) are often a flaw in cheese, a red flag that something's gone awry. Consequently, brassicas are often passed over for pairings—but they shouldn't be.

A couple of tips for preparing cauliflower chips: use a sharp knife, the stem is your friend, and there will be some collateral damage. Toss the "waste" into a salad the next day, as penance for the decadence previously wrought.

Preheat the oven to 250°F. Line a baking sheet with parchment paper.

Trim the stem of **1 cauliflower head** so that the cauliflower stands level on the stem. Trim off the leaves. Quarter the head, using the stem as the dissection point. With a very sharp knife, cut each quarter into ⅛-inch-thick slices, so that the stem and florets remain attached—they'll look like little tree silhouettes. They won't all be intact or perfect, but that's okay.

Lay the slices in a single layer on the prepared baking sheet. Lightly brush with **1 teaspoon olive oil**, then turn and brush with another **teaspoon of olive oil**. Season with **kosher salt** and **white pepper**. Bake until crisp and toasted, 1½ to 2 hours. These are best right out of the oven, so bake them while preparing the lotus root and carrot chips.

Makes 1 cup. Also great with **Brie Fermier Jouvence** (see page 28) and **Brebirousse D'Argental** (see page 50) .

Joseph Drouhin Meursault

Chardonnay grapes, Meursault, Burgundy, France

Full body with notes of honey, hazelnut, plum, and chamomile

An elegant, muscular, rich, entry-level white Burgundy from an iconic chateau. Creamy, oak vibes hold up to the formidable strength of Époisses.

Duchesse de Bourgogne

Flanders Red Ale, Vichte, Belgium

Light/medium body, sour, with notes of apple cider vinegar, cherry, and vanilla

Sour beers pair especially well with rich, creamy cheeses like Époisses; their astringent quality powers through the intense butterfat. Tangy, sweet, yeasty tones highlight the yeastiness of the cheese.

BREBIROUSSE D'ARGENTAL
Pasteurized Sheep's Milk
Lyon, France

ROASTED ROMANESCO WITH TARRAGON

OSSAU IRATY VIEILLE
Raw Sheep's Milk
Aquitaine, France

BANANA-MANGO CHUTNEY

OLD CHATHAM SHEEPHERDING COMPANY EWE'S BLUE
Pasteurized Sheep's Milk
Old Chatham, New York

HOT CAKES SMOKED CHOCOLATE CHIPS

EWEPHORIC

The animal notes of sheep's milk impart a unique character to cheese across styles and nations: the smell of an old wool blanket hanging on a barn door, the taste of hay carried in the dusty wind, the sweetness of scalded milk—often described simply as "sheepy." These three cheeses couldn't be more distinct—creamy and mild, hard and aged, blue—yet each expresses the pleasures of sheep's milk in its own special way.

BREBIROUSSE D'ARGENTAL

Notes of sweet cream and roasted sunchokes, with a soft, creamy paste and washed/bloomy rind

Annato-tinged Brebirousse d'Argental has gentle vegetal/nutty notes pervading a rich paste of lingering sheepy sweetness. Mild and milky, it's a fine choice for a relaxed first date with sheep's milk cheese.

ROASTED ROMANESCO WITH TARRAGON

You'll need romanesco, extra-virgin olive oil, rice vinegar, fresh tarragon

Romanesco is a bright green, cauliflower-esque vegetable that looks fantastic on a cheese plate. Seasoned with rice vinegar and fresh tarragon and finished with good olive oil, it highlights the vegetal/herbal notes in Brebirousse d'Argental, while adding acidity and cratered texture to contrast its creaminess.

Preheat the oven to 450°F.

Trim **1 romanesco head** into bite-size florets and toss with **¼ cup olive oil** and **1 teaspoon rice vinegar**. Season with salt and pepper. Spread the romanesco over a baking sheet and roast for 10 minutes. Stir and roast for 10 to 15 minutes more, until tender but still firm. Remove from the oven and toss with **1 tablespoon fresh tarragon leaves**. Taste and adjust the seasoning, and drizzle with a bit more **extra-virgin olive oil**. Serve warm or at room temperature.

Makes 1 cup. Tasty paired with **Langres** (see page 106). Great in a salad the next day, with raisins, pine nuts, and some **fresh cheese** (see page 23 to 24).

OSSAU IRATY VIEILLE

Notes of tea biscuit, brown butter, and caramelized banana with a firm, smooth paste and natural rind

Ossau Iraty is France's most iconic aged sheep's milk cheese, produced in a bastion of sheep-cheese making: the Pyrénées Mountains. Matured for approximately nine months, Ossau has the benchmark traits of its style: It's grassy, nutty, buttery, and caramelized, with lanolin undertones.

BANANA-MANGO CHUTNEY

You'll need unsalted butter, yellow onion, jalapeño, garlic, fresh ginger, white wine vinegar, mango, banana, brown sugar, curry powder

This sweet and savory chutney plays on the caramelized flavors and smooth paste of Ossau Iraty, which benefits from the silky pull of banana, tropical sweetness of mango, and punctuating complexity of curry spice.

In a medium saucepan, melt **1 tablespoon butter** over medium heat until foaming. Add **½ cup diced yellow onion** and **1 tablespoon minced seeded jalapeño** and cook until the onion is translucent and just beginning to brown at the edges, 5 to 6 minutes. Add **1 minced garlic clove**, **1 tablespoon minced fresh ginger**, and **2 tablespoons white wine vinegar** and cook until the vinegar has been absorbed. Add **1 diced peeled mango**, **1 diced banana**, **1 tablespoon brown sugar**, **1 teaspoon curry powder**, and a **pinch of salt** and stir to combine. Add **¼ cup water**, bring to a boil, then reduce the heat to low and cook until the liquid has evaporated, about 10 minutes.

Makes 1 cup. Best served the same day. Sidles up nicely to **Berkswell** (see page 98).

OLD CHATHAM SHEEPHERDING COMPANY EWE'S BLUE

Notes of buttermilk biscuit, tofu, and seaweed, with a semi-firm, creamy paste

Ewe's Blue is one of the few sheep's milk blues produced in the United States. Its fruity/tangy character is similar to Roquefort, though milder and less salty.

Hot Cakes Smoked Chocolate Chips are made from organic, semisweet chocolate that has been cold-smoked over alderwood. The sweet, fruity, smoked cacao flavors of these bite-size morsels play especially well against the sheepy and fruity/tangy notes of Ewe's Blue. Delicious with **Barely Buzzed** (see page 154) and **Shakerag Blue** (see page 91). A fun substitution for plain chocolate chips in **Ritz Cracker–Bacon Brickle** (see page 174).

BERRIED TREASURE

A creamy puck of luscious California Brie is draped in kataifi—butter-crisped strands of crunchy Greek pastry. Surprising herb and spice combinations elevate three distinctive fruity accompaniments, the berries' sweet, high-tone acidity in service to the buttery baked Brie. This is a high-impact, low-effort dish, served communally for a buffet lunch or in individual portions for a sit-down dinner party.

RASPBERRY-LICORICE COMPOTE

PICKLED BLUEBERRIES WITH GINGER & STAR ANISE

MACERATED STRAWBERRIES WITH SHISO & BLACK PEPPER

MARIN FRENCH CHEESE
TRADITIONAL BRIE

Pasteurized Cow's Milk
Petaluma, California

MARIN FRENCH CHEESE TRADITIONAL BRIE

Notes of button mushroom and buttered bread crumbs, with a creamy paste and white bloomy rind

You could eat Marin French Cheese Traditional Brie out of the package and have a completely satisfying experience. It's everything you'd expect in a well-made Brie: creamy, buttery paste encased in a velvety, mushroom-y rind. It's a particularly shrewd choice for a baked cheese course, as it's not so precious or expensive that cooking it is an unconscionable sacrifice.

Marin French "Traditional Brie" is 8 ounces, enough for four people as an appetizer or light dessert. The "Petite Crème" is a 4-ounce triple-crème: creamier than the Traditional Brie but lovely in this recipe as a decadent single-serving dessert. To make the "petite" version, use the same amount of kataifi and butter and make eight bunches instead of two. You'll have less for wrapping, but since the cheese is so rich, that's okay. Good-quality kataifi can be purchased at specialty Greek or European grocers.

BAKED BRIE KATAIFI

You'll need kataifi, salted butter, Brie

Remove the kataifi from the freezer 1 hour prior to preparation, keeping it in its plastic packaging while tempering to prevent its drying out. Preheat the oven to 425°F. Line a baking sheet with parchment paper.

In a small saucepan, melt **4 tablespoons butter** until foaming. Skim the foam from the surface. Brush a thin layer of the melted butter over the prepared baking sheet.

Divide **6 ounces kataifi** into two bunches, carefully separating the strands of pastry to minimize breakage (some strands will still break—that's okay). Place one bunch horizontally on the baking sheet, spreading out the strands of the pastry to ¼ inch thick. Place the second bunch on top, perpendicular to the first, forming an X, and spread it out in the same fashion as the first bunch.

Set the **Brie** in the center of the X. Bring each section of kataifi up over the Brie, gathering it at the top. Gently fan out the strands around the cheese and twist the gathered ends into a knot on top. Brush the entire surface of the pastry with melted butter. Bake for about 25 minutes, rotating the pan once, until the pastry is golden brown. Serve immediately, with accompaniments on the side.

MACERATED STRAWBERRIES WITH SHISO & BLACK PEPPER
You'll need honey, orange, bitters, strawberries, shiso leaves

A common Japanese herb, shiso has a profound cinnamon-like quality and is an easy swap for basil or mint. It adds a complex herbal note to strawberries, enlivened with orange, a dash of bitters, and freshly ground black pepper. This chilled herbal/floral salad contrasts the warm, buttery *kataifi* pastry and oozing, melted Brie.

In a medium nonreactive bowl, whisk together **2 tablespoons honey**, the **zest of 1 orange**, **1 tablespoon fresh orange juice**, **2 or 3 dashes bitters** (such as **Peychaud's** or **Angostura**), and **¼ teaspoon kosher salt**. Add **2 cups halved trimmed strawberries** and toss gently to coat.

Macerate in the refrigerator for at least 3 hours, or up to 12 (or overnight). A half hour before serving, toss with a **chiffonade of 5 shiso leaves** and add a **few cracks of black pepper**. Refrigerate until ready to serve.

Makes 2½ cups. Also a great match with **Bijou** (see page 36) and **Leonora** (see page 115).

RASPBERRY-LICORICE COMPOTE
You'll need lemon, raspberries, unsalted butter, licorice root, vanilla bean, sugar, Pernod

Raspberries love licorice root: Its anise-like flavor ramps up the sweet and tart raspberries and is then picked up again by Pernod. Licorice root has its own unique sweetness—procuring it is worth a trip to your local spice shop. This bright fuchsia compote scissors through the richness of the Brie and pastry.

Peel **2 strips of lemon peel** with a vegetable peeler. Divide **1 pint fresh raspberries in half**.

In a medium sauté pan, melt **1 tablespoon butter** over medium heat until foaming. Add **1 licorice root** (broken in half if too big for the pan), cook for 1 minute, then add half the raspberries, the lemon peel, and **1 split vanilla bean**. Cook for 2 minutes. Add **¼ cup sugar** and **¼ teaspoon kosher salt** and cook until the raspberries release their juices and begin to break down, about 2 minutes more. Add **1 tablespoon Pernod** and cook, shaking the pan gently, for 3 to 4 minutes. Stir once or twice, reduce the heat to low, cover, and cook for 5 minutes. Remove from the heat and add the remaining raspberries and a **crack of black pepper**. Cool to room temperature, remove and discard the licorice root, lemon peel, and vanilla bean, and serve.

Makes 1½ cups. Store in an airtight container in the refrigerator for up to 2 days. Wouldn't kick **Goat Camembert** (see page 83) or **Roquefort** (see page 29) out of bed.

PICKLED BLUEBERRIES WITH GINGER & STAR ANISE

You'll need blueberries, lemon, fresh ginger, sugar, apple cider vinegar, cinnamon stick, star anise, vanilla bean

Pickling draws out the wet earth notes of blueberries without impinging on their sweetness. Ginger and star anise provide a spiced background for the interplay of acidity and fat in this pairing.

Divide **1 pint blueberries** into two glass pint jars. Peel **1 lemon** with a vegetable peeler. Cut **1 thumb-size piece peeled fresh ginger** into 3 or 4 discs.

In a small saucepan, combine **1 cup water**, **½ cup sugar**, **1 cup apple cider vinegar**, **1 cinnamon stick**, **5 star anise**, the lemon peel, **1 split vanilla bean**, and the ginger and bring to a boil. Reduce the heat to low and simmer for 5 minutes. Remove from the heat, remove and discard the vanilla bean, and cool for 5 minutes. Pour over the blueberries, ensuring each jar gets an equal amount of lemon peel and star anise. Cool to room temperature. Make a loose ball of plastic wrap and place it over the blueberries to keep the blueberries submerged in the liquid; repeat with the second jar.

Makes 2 pints, including the pickling liquid. Store in the refrigerator for up to 3 weeks. Delicious paired with **Cabra al Vino** (see page 154). Also a fun addition to a salad.

DRINK ME

Cleto Chiarli "Vecchia Modena" Lambrusco di Sorbara

Sorbara grapes, Emilia-Romagna, Italy
Medium-body sparkler with notes of wild strawberry, raspberry, and mint

This flirty lambrusco is pretty close to a perfect pairing, with a creamy, bright effervescence that cuts through the richness of the Brie while reinforcing the fruity/floral tones of the berry accompaniments.

ANTON'S LIEBE BLOND
Pasteurized Cow's Milk
Allgau, Germany

BORSCHTMALLOWS

CHEESE IS FOR LOVERS

Say it with an enchanting plate of creamy, sensual, love-themed cheeses paired with sweet, surprising accompaniments. This aphrodisiacal flight can take it to the next level or remind a special someone they're all that and a plate of cheese.

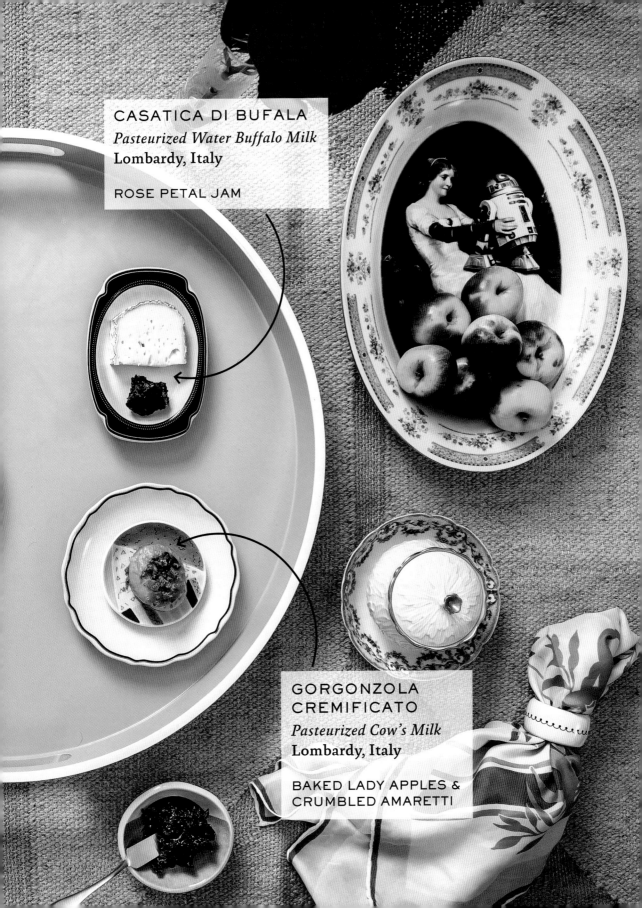

CASATICA DI BUFALA
Pasteurized Water Buffalo Milk
Lombardy, Italy

ROSE PETAL JAM

**GORGONZOLA
CREMIFICATO**
Pasteurized Cow's Milk
Lombardy, Italy

BAKED LADY APPLES &
CRUMBLED AMARETTI

ANTON'S LIEBE BLOND
Notes of cultured butter and button mushrooms, with a creamy, pliable paste and white bloomy rind

Maybe blondes do have more fun? Anton's Liebe Blond (that's "Blond Love" in German) embodies the clean flavors indicative of excellent milk and capable cheese making. A straightforward, mild square of creamy, slightly salty deliciousness.

BORSCHTMALLOWS
You'll need unflavored gelatin, beet powder, granulated sugar, light corn syrup, cornstarch, confectioners' sugar, dried dill, nonstick cooking spray

These beet-inflected pink marshmallows dotted with dill are a whimsical treat based on the flavors of a classic vegetable soup; the cheese plays the role of sour cream.

Place **1¼-ounce package unflavored gelatin, 1 tablespoon beet powder** (I used **Starwest Botanicals Organic Beetroot Powder**), and **⅓ cup water** in the bowl of a stand mixer fitted with a whisk attachment.

In a small saucepan, combine **½ cup water, ½ cup plus 1 tablespoon sugar, ⅓ cup corn syrup**, and **¼ teaspoon kosher salt**, cover, and cook over medium-high heat until the mixture reaches 240°F on a candy thermometer, about 7 to 8 minutes. Remove from the heat.

With the mixer on low, slowly stream the sugar syrup into the gelatin mixture (avoid the whisk). Increase the speed to high and whisk until the batter is lukewarm, thick, and looks like pulled taffy, about 10 minutes.

Meanwhile, combine **¼ cup cornstarch** and **¼ cup confectioners' sugar** in a small bowl. Spray a loaf pan with **nonstick cooking spray** and dust the bottom and sides with some of the cornstarch mixture. Sprinkle **1 teaspoon dried dill** over the bottom of the pan.

Working quickly, pour the marshmallow mixture into the prepared pan and spread it evenly with a lightly oiled spatula (or pipe from a pastry bag—see **Matcha Marshmallows**, page 65). Dust the surface again with some of the cornstarch mixture and **1 teaspoon dried dill**. Let sit, uncovered, for at least 4 hours or up to overnight.

Turn the marshmallow block out onto a cutting board and cut into twelve 1-inch squares with a pizza wheel. Lightly dust the sides of each marshmallow with the remaining cornstarch mixture.

Makes 12. Store between sheets of parchment paper in an airtight container in a cool, dry place for up to 3 weeks. Also yummy with some of the youthful goat cheeses in this book, including **Valançay** (see page 65), **Bijou** (see page 36), and **Goat Camembert** (see page 83).

CASATICA DI BUFALA
Notes of vanilla pudding and sandstone, with a custardy paste and white bloomy rind

Seducing with its rich sweetness, Casatica di Bufala utilizes its buffalo milk wiles (see **Buffalo Soldiers**, page 68) to charming effect. A beautifully tended rind adds earthy funk to this supple cheese.

Rose Petal Jam is a bracing preserve, both in terms of sweetness and concentrated rose flavor. There are French, American, and Indian producers of this seasonal, wildcard condiment. If you happen to spot it, snag a jar for your pantry. A little goes a long way.

GORGONZOLA CREMIFICATO
Notes of fresh hay and grape syrup, with a creamy, spreadable paste and natural rind

As its name suggests, Gorgonzola Cremificato is the creamiest iteration of this famous mountain blue cheese. Consider its sweet, earthy/fruity/barnyard notes a study in creamy butterfat as a delivery system for intense flavor.

BAKED LADY APPLES WITH GORGONZOLA CREMIFICATO & CRUMBLED AMARETTI
You'll need unsalted butter, Lady apples (or another small apple variety), Gorgonzala Cremificato, red wine, cinnamon stick, Amaretti cookies

Sometimes the best place for a cheese is inside its accompaniment. These wee baked Lady apples are sweet and tart and a fetching presentation for the silken, funky decadence that is Gorgonzola Cremificato. If you have a hard time finding Gorgonzola Cremificato, substitute Gorgonzola Dolce.

Preheat the oven to 350°F. **Butter** a loaf pan.

Core and make a ½-inch-wide hollow in **4 Lady apples**. Divide **2 ounces Gorgonzola Cremificato** among the four apples and stand them in the prepared pan hollow-side up. Add **¼ cup red wine** and **1 cinnamon stick**.

Cover with aluminum foil and bake until the apples are tender, about 30 minutes, then turn the oven to broil, uncover, and broil until the apples are browned, about 5 minutes. Crumble **8 small Amaretti cookies** and measure out ¼ cup of the crumbs. Remove the apples from the pan, plate them, sprinkle with the cookie crumbs (about 1 tablespoon each), and serve.

Makes 4.

CHABICHOU
Pasteurized Goat's Milk
Poitou, France

**PINK PEPPERCORN
LYCHEE**

JOIE DE CHÈVRE

The joy of eating a perfect bite of French goat cheese. Terroir-driven jewels of young goaty gloriousness aren't just a food in France—they're a cultural birthright. Pure, clean milk and deft affinage craft exemplary cheeses serving as inspiration for cheese makers and cheese lovers alike. Accompaniments parlay Asian flavors—the tannins of green tea, the floral sweetness of lychee, and warming tandoori spices—into exciting companions that coax citrus and earth notes from the cheese.

VALENÇAY
Pasteurized Goat's Milk
Loire Valley, France

MATCHA MARSHMALLOWS

BÛCHERON
Pasteurized Goat's Milk
Poitou-Charentes, France

TANDOORI CASHEWS

CHABICHOU

Notes of bacon fat, hay, and chamomile, with a dense, creamy paste and wrinkled
Geotrichum *rind*

Wrinkles can be sexy! A brainy, pale golden rind encases a fudgy core inching toward an oozing creamline. Lighter floral/grassy flavors balance savory roasted meat notes in this diminutive drum.

PINK PEPPERCORN LYCHEE

You'll need fresh lychee, pink peppercorns

The floral undertones of **fresh lychee** coax more of the same from the Chabichou, and its silky texture plays well against the cheese's rich paste. Peel and pit each lychee and roll in **crushed pink peppercorns** for an easy and exotic accompaniment. Pairs beautifully with **Fresh Crottin** and **Bijou** (see page 36).

VALENÇAY

Notes of Greek yogurt, oyster shells, and honey, with a fluffy, moist paste and ashed rind

This pyramid-shaped stunner from the Loire Valley, goat cheese capital of the world, is surprisingly complex given its youth. Valençay tastes like a spring garden smells after it rains: Heady earthy/vegetal and tangy/mineral notes abound.

MATCHA MARSHMALLOWS

You'll need unflavored gelatin, culinary-grade matcha powder, granulated sugar, light corn syrup, lemon extract, cornstarch, confectioners' sugar, nonstick cooking spray

Matcha's mild tannins contribute a mellow, vegetal acidity alongside Valençay's bright, citrus tones. Tea-grade matcha powder can be quite expensive—go with culinary grade here.

Place **1 (¼-ounce) package unflavored gelatin, 1 tablespoon matcha powder,** and **⅓ cup water** in the bowl of a stand mixer fitted with a whisk attachment.

In a small saucepan, combine **½ cup water, ½ cup plus 1 tablespoon granulated sugar, ⅓ cup light corn syrup,** and **¼ teaspoon kosher salt,** cover, and cook over medium-high heat until the mixture reaches 240°F on a candy thermometer, about 7 to 8 minutes. Remove from the heat.

With the mixer on low, slowly stream the sugar syrup into the gelatin mixture (avoid the whisk). Increase the speed to high and whisk until the batter is lukewarm, thick, and looks like pulled taffy, about 10 minutes. Add **¼ teaspoon lemon extract** during the last minute of whipping.

Meanwhile, combine **¼ cup cornstarch** and **¼ cup confectioners' sugar** in a small bowl. Line a baking sheet with parchment paper and lightly dust with some of the cornstarch mixture.

Working quickly, pour the marshmallow mixture into a piping bag fitted with a medium round tip and pipe the marshmallow batter onto the baking sheet (for cubes, see **Borschtmallows**, page 60). Dust the tops lightly again with some of the cornstarch mixture. Let sit uncovered for at least 4 hours or up to overnight.

Makes at least 12. Store between sheets of parchment paper in an airtight container in a cool, dry place for up to 3 weeks. Also yummy with **La Tur** (see page 106). Great for s'mores, hot chocolate, or puffed rice treats.

BÛCHERON
Notes of cultured butter, oyster crackers, and eucalyptus, with a chalky, rich paste and white bloomy rind

Bûcheron straddles the line between youth and maturity. It's the most mature cheese in the flight, and the most robust. Sometimes Bûcheron can overwhelm the palate with acidic piquancy, but when it's handled adroitly, it's bright, nutty, and gamy with a rich, mouth-coating paste.

TANDOORI CASHEWS
You'll need egg white, ground ginger, cumin, coriander, paprika, turmeric, clove, nutmeg, cinnamon, white pepper, sugar, cashews

Tandoori spice is a great addition to the crunchy, salty, sweet, and savory trope of spiced nuts. The creaminess of cashew and the warming tandoori spices make these nuts a versatile accompaniment that pairs well with many cheeses. Bûcheron benefits from the creamy quality of cashews, and the spices temper the potentially aggressive acidity of the cheese.

Preheat the oven to 300°F.

Beat **1 egg white** until soft and foamy and set aside.

In a medium bowl, whisk together **2 teaspoons ground ginger, 2 teaspoons ground cumin, 1 teaspoon ground coriander, 1 teaspoon paprika, 1 teaspoon ground turmeric, ½ teaspoon ground cloves, ½ teaspoon freshly grated nutmeg, ½ teaspoon ground cinnamon, ½ teaspoon freshly ground white pepper, ½ teaspoon kosher salt,** and **½ cup sugar**. Whisk in the egg white until thoroughly combined. Stir in **1½ cups unsalted roasted cashews** and mix until evenly coated.

Spread the cashews in a single layer on a baking sheet and bake for about 20 minutes, until the nuts are medium brown. Remove from the oven, toss, and stir. Cool in the pan on a wire rack—the cashews will crisp as they cool. Break the nuts apart before serving or storing.

Makes 1½ cups. Store in an airtight container in a cool, dry place for up to 1 month. Wouldn't kick **Fat Bottom Girl** (see page 125), **Mahon** (see page 116), or **Goudas** (see page 126) out of bed.

DRINK ME

Champalou Vouvray Brut Méthode Traditionelle

Chenin Blanc grapes, Loire Valley, France

Medium-body sparkling, with notes of beeswax, wet wool, and lemon curd

Clos Huet Vouvray Sec

Chenin Blanc grapes, Loire Valley, France

Medium body, with notes of stone fruit, honey, lemon, and wet stone

Vouvray is one of the signature white wines of the Loire Valley, home to many of the most iconic French goat cheeses. They're crisp, high-acid whites, with subtle fruit and mineral charms. Both sparkling and still iterations serve this flight well.

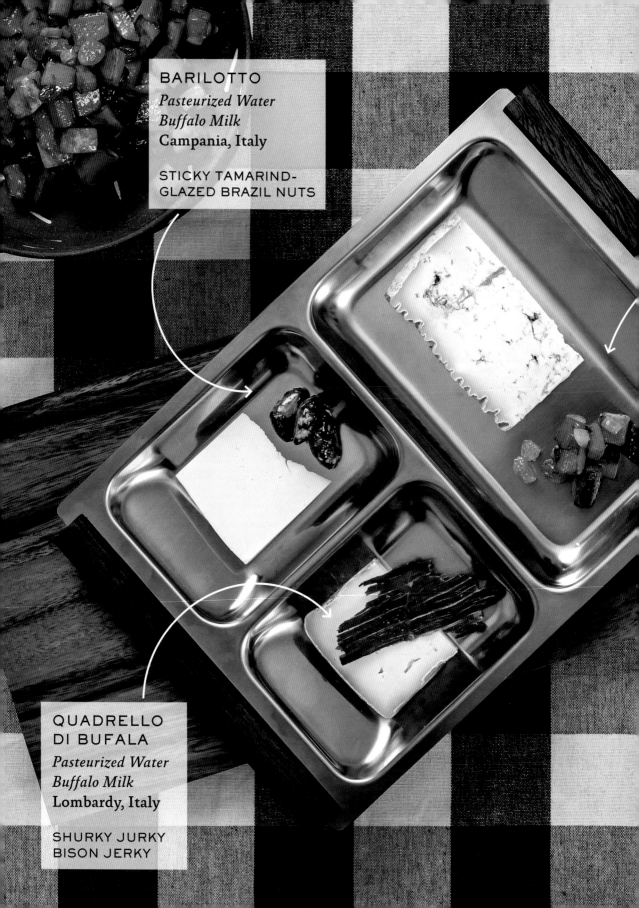

BARILOTTO
Pasteurized Water
Buffalo Milk
Campania, Italy

STICKY TAMARIND-
GLAZED BRAZIL NUTS

QUADRELLO
DI BUFALA
Pasteurized Water
Buffalo Milk
Lombardy, Italy

SHURKY JURKY
BISON JERKY

BLU DI BUFALA

*Pasteurized Water
Buffalo Milk*
Lombardy, Italy

BUTTERNUT
SQUASH &
GOLDEN RAISIN
CHUTNEY

BUFFALO SOLDIERS

Water buffalo milk is God's custard, and
it makes heavenly cheese. Rich, sweet,
and bone-white, it's nutrient dense with
more fat and protein than cow's milk,
with a clean, lactic sweetness that's
entirely unique. Tart accompaniments
are de rigueur here; the buffalo milk
appreciates the tangy interruption.

BARILOTTO

Notes of melted vanilla ice cream and salt water, with an ultra-smooth, pliable paste

Barilotto is a straightforward cheese with a texture similar to ricotta salata. Made from the leftover whey of **Mozarella di Bufala Campana** (see page 168) production, it has a compact creaminess and a clean, briny finish. What Barilotto lacks in flash it makes up for with sweet, simple, milky charm.

STICKY TAMARIND-GLAZED BRAZIL NUTS

You'll need sugar, tamarind concentrate, soy sauce, ancho chile powder, Brazil nuts

Brazil nuts are creamy and high in fat, with a mouthfeel so similar to Barilotto that they're an intuitive, natural pairing. Tamarind adds a fruity, sour slant, a punctuation of the rich nut and cheese, while ancho lends smokiness more than heat. The finished nuts are quite sticky—an interesting textural contribution to the pairing.

Preheat the oven to 300°F. Line a baking sheet with parchment paper.

In a medium bowl, whisk together **2 tablespoons sugar, 1 teaspoon tamarind concentrate, 1 teaspoon soy sauce, ½ teaspoon ancho chile powder**, and **¼ teaspoon kosher salt**. Add **1 cup raw Brazil nuts** and stir to coat. Pour the nuts onto the prepared baking sheet and bake for 12 to 15 minutes, keeping an eye on them in the last couple of minutes to ensure they don't burn. Give the nuts a stir and cool completely before serving.

Makes 1 cup. Store in an airtight container in a cool, dry place for up to 2 days. Also a great match with **Goat Gouda** (see page 128).

QUADRELLO DI BUFALA

Notes of crème fraîche and mushroom broth, with a silky, semi-firm paste and mottled washed/natural rind

Quadrello di Bufala's rich paste bares clean, earthy, sweet notes that linger and evolve, with a complex, creamy salinity reminiscent of lobster bisque. It's often compared to Taleggio, and while it's true that both cheeses are washed in brine, semi-firm, and square, Quadrello is subtler than its funky cow's milk cousin.

Shurky Jurky Bison Jerky is made from American bison, a "buffalo" related to the water buffalo that produce the milk used in these cheeses. The marinade for the jerky includes pineapple and a Worcestershire-style sauce that lends tangy, sweet notes to the jerky, which plays well with the mineral and earth notes in the cheese. The chewiness of the jerky is an interesting contrast to the smooth, creamy Quadrello di Bufala.

BLU DI BUFALA
Notes of hazelnut, dandelion, and iron, with a fudgy, firm paste and natural rind

The custardy quality of buffalo milk is well suited to blue cheese: The richness runs interference with the powerful flavors of the blue mold. Sweet, mineral notes abound in Blu di Bufala, with roasted vegetal undertones. Like eating a funky vegetable potpie.

BUTTERNUT SQUASH & GOLDEN RAISIN CHUTNEY
You'll need olive oil, yellow onion, garlic, bay leaf, butternut squash, fresh thyme, sugar, red wine vinegar, golden raisins

Heat **2 tablespoons olive oil** in a medium sauté pan over medium heat until fragrant. Add **½ cup diced yellow onion**, **1 garlic clove**, and **1 bay leaf** and sauté until the onion is translucent and browned around the edges. Transfer to a plate, discarding the bay leaf.

Heat **1 tablespoon olive oil** in the same pan over medium-high heat. Add **2 cups ½-inch-dice peeled butternut squash** and **2 sprigs of thyme** and cook, stirring only occasionally so that the squash browns, for about 15 minutes. Season with salt and pepper.

Return the onion mixture to the pan and cook for a minute or two. Add **1 tablespoon sugar**, **2 tablespoons red wine vinegar**, and **¼ cup golden raisins** and cook, stirring, until the sugar and vinegar thicken into a glaze. Remove from the heat, remove and discard the thyme and garlic, taste, and adjust the seasoning. Serve warm or at room temperature.

Makes 1½ cups. Best served the same day. Delicious paired with **Ossau Iraty Vieille** (see page 50) and **Smoked Ricotta** (see page 146). Tasty tossed in a kale salad or alongside pork chops.

SELLES-SUR-CHER
Pasteurized Goat's Milk
Centre, France

PISTACHIO PESTO &
QUICK-PICKLED CHERRIES

ASHES TO ASHES
The striking contrast between the bright white paste of goat cheese and blue/gray ash is visually intriguing, but it's not the whole story. Ash plays an important role—especially in goat-cheese making—of protecting the surface of the cheese during maturation, balancing the pH, and wicking excess moisture. Serve when you're hankering to move beyond the surface of things.

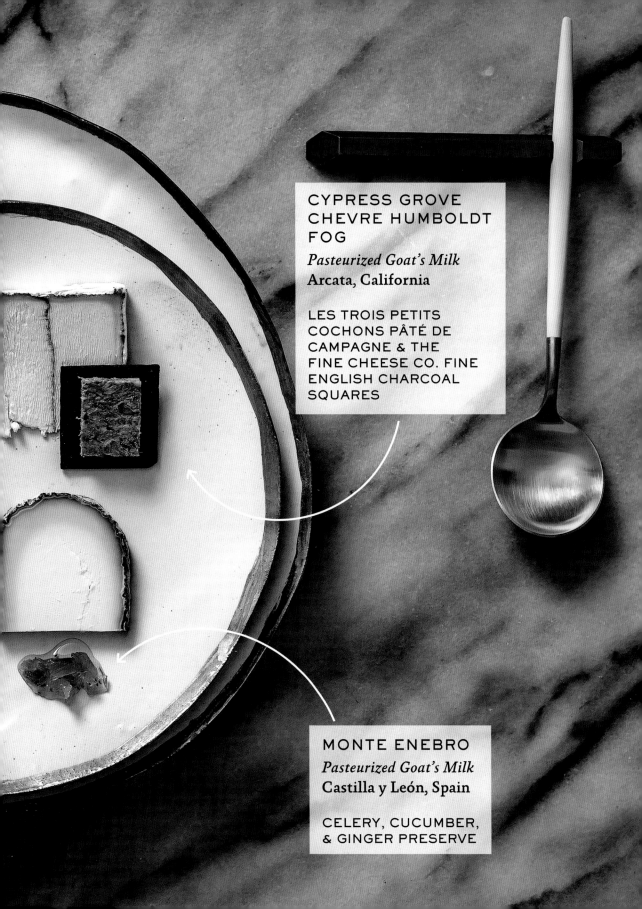

CYPRESS GROVE CHEVRE HUMBOLDT FOG
Pasteurized Goat's Milk
Arcata, California

LES TROIS PETITS COCHONS PÂTÉ DE CAMPAGNE & THE FINE CHEESE CO. FINE ENGLISH CHARCOAL SQUARES

MONTE ENEBRO
Pasteurized Goat's Milk
Castilla y León, Spain

CELERY, CUCUMBER, & GINGER PRESERVE

SELLES-SUR-CHER
Notes of kefir, mascarpone, and wildflower honey, with a moist, cakey paste and delicate ashed rind

Selles-sur-Cher is a classic beaut from the Loire Valley, the cradle of French goat-cheese making. This small, round puck is dusted in ash and matured for three to five weeks, resulting in an elegant, delicious chèvre with lemon, green almond, and mineral notes. Young Selles-sur-Cher is moist and cakey; more mature rounds can soften into a melted ice cream–y ooze.

PISTACHIO PESTO & QUICK-PICKLED CHERRIES
You'll need pistachios, lemon, fennel pollen, extra-virgin olive oil, cherries, sherry vinegar, sugar, orange, cinnamon stick, allspice berries

Pistachios add color, crunch, and an additional layer of richness to Selles-sur-Cher. Pickled cherries perk things up with a tart sweetness.

For the pistachio pesto:
In a food processor, combine **1 cup shelled dry-roasted pistachios**, the **zest and juice of 1 lemon**, **¼ teaspoon kosher salt**, and **¼ teaspoon fennel pollen** and pulse until finely chopped into a paste. With the motor running, slowly drizzle in **¼ cup extra-virgin olive oil** until combined.

Transfer the pesto to a container, cover, and let the flavors marry overnight. Serve at room temperature.

Makes ¾ cup. Store in the refrigerator for up to 1 week. Also a great match with **Cayuga Blue** (see page 179). Excellent slathered on a piece of broiled mild fish.

For the pickled cherries:
Place **24 halved pitted cherries** in a glass pint jar. In a small saucepan, combine **¼ cup sherry vinegar**, **¼ cup sugar**, **¼ cup water**, the **zest and juice of ½ orange**, **1 cinnamon stick**, and **1 teaspoon allspice berries** and bring to a boil over medium-high heat. Reduce the heat to low and simmer for 2 to 3 minutes, then pour the pickling liquid into the jar over the cherries. Cool to room temperature, then make a loose ball of plastic wrap and place it over the cherries to keep the cherries submerged. Seal tightly and refrigerate until ready to serve.

Makes 1 pint. Store in the refrigerator for up to 2 weeks. Also keen on **Ewe's Blue** (see page 51). Yummy as a cocktail garnish.

CYPRESS GROVE CHEVRE HUMBOLDT FOG

Notes of oyster crackers and buttered mushrooms, with a fluffy, creamy paste and white bloomy rind

Humboldt Fog is a popular "gateway" cheese for many enthusiasts. Maybe it's the first American artisanal cheese they ever ate, or the first goat cheese they liked—either way, it deserves respect for its groundbreaking role in the American cheese scene. It's a balanced expression of bright, fluffy goat's milk, and an accessible, satisfying choice.

Les Trois Petits Cochon Organic Pâté de Campagne stays true to the essentials of a rustic country pâté: coarsely ground pork, Cognac, garlic, onions, allspice, cloves, and white pepper. Delicious with **Fat Bottom Girl** (see page 125) and **Saint-Nectaire** (see page 41).

The Fine Cheese Co. Fine English Charcoal Squares are a wink to the ash theme of the flight. Buttery, mild, and distinctive looking, they're a perfect vehicle for a slice of Humboldt Fog and pâté.

MONTE ENEBRO

Notes of black walnut, roasted red pepper skins, and chorizo, with a dense, fudgy paste and robust ashed rind

Monte Enebro is a goat cheese for people who like blue cheese, a funky, peppery expression of tangy goat's milk.

CELERY, CUCUMBER, & GINGER PRESERVE
You'll need celery, cucumber, sugar, fresh ginger, lemon, lime, celery seed

This preserve honors celery's crisp texture and sweet, vegetal character. Cucumber adds fresh tones; ginger, zing that answers Monte Enebro's aggressive tang.

In a medium heavy-bottomed saucepan, combine **1 pound diced celery, 1 pound peeled, seeded, shredded cucumber, 1½ cups sugar, ½ cup water, 2 tablespoons minced fresh ginger, 1 teaspoon lemon zest, 2 tablespoons fresh lemon juice, 1 teaspoon lime zest, 2 tablespoons fresh lime juice,** and **¼ teaspoon kosher salt.** Cook over medium heat, stirring occasionally, until the liquid has almost completely evaporated, about 1½ hours.

Remove from the heat and add **½ teaspoon celery seed**. Pour into two glass half-pint jars, cool to room temperature, cover tightly, and store in the refrigerator until ready to serve.

Makes 1 pint. Store in the refrigerator for up to 1 week. Also a great match with **Brebis Blanche** (see page 24). Tasty on cream cheese sandwiches or slathered on crusty, dark bread with **Summer Sausage** (see page 138) and **Caerphilly** (see page 98).

BELGIAN BEAUTS

There's perfection in simplicity when it comes to Belgian cheese, where Dutch, French, and monastic traditions meet. They aren't always easy to find in the United States, but they're worth seeking out, as their unique elegance requires little adornment: fresh, savory, sweet, and piquant pairings waltz gently in step, allowing the cheese to shine.

LE CHARMOIX
Pasteurized Cow's Milk
Maffe, Belgium

CHARRED SCALLIONS
WITH MIKE'S
HOT HONEY

LE WAVREUMONT
Raw Cow's Milk
Werbomont, Belgium

PICCALILLI

GREVENBROEKER
*Raw Cow's Milk,
Hamont-Achel*
Flanders, Belgium

ROASTED CONCORD
GRAPES WITH THYME

LE CHARMOIX

Notes of sour cream and chive, with a rich, cakey paste and yellow-hued washed rind

Briny, yeasty Le Charmoix is a textural wonder, with a paste like dense cheesecake. It has milky, hazelnut flavors in its youth, but chive and stone fruit notes emerge with more maturity.

CHARRED SCALLIONS WITH MIKE'S HOT HONEY

You'll need high-heat oil such as canola, grapeseed, or peanut oil, scallions, Mike's Hot Honey

Scallions are a natural partner for Le Charmoix. Mike's Hot Honey adds a spicy sweetness that plays well against the mild funk of the cheese. Use just a drizzle of honey—it's quite fiery. Feel free to substitute a non-spiced honey: a light, floral, orange-blossom honey works best.

Heat a large cast-iron pan (if you have a cast-iron grill pan, even better) over medium-high heat until the pan is very hot and starting to smoke. Add enough **oil** to lightly coat the pan and raise the heat to high. Add **4 trimmed scallions** and sear, turning every 3 minutes or so, until glossy and charred.

Serve 1 scallion per cheese plate. Drizzle each scallion with **Mike's Hot Honey**. *Makes 4.* Also yummy with **Red Hawk** (see page 158).

LE WAVREUMONT

Notes of fresh ham and vegetable peels, with a smooth, firm paste and washed rind

Wavreumont is tangy and buttery, with just a whisper of funk. Clean milk and precise production are the name of the game here; this appealing cheese manages to present familiar flavors in a complex fashion.

PICCALILLI

You'll need extra-virgin olive oil, yellow onion, fresh ginger, garlic, bay leaf, oregano, fenugreek seeds, turmeric, cloves, red bell pepper, celery, cauliflower, zucchini, sugar, apple cider vinegar, frozen peas

Piccalilli, a sweet and sour mix of spiced vegetables, lends a ham-and-pickle-sandwich vibe to meaty Wavreumont.

Heat **2 tablespoons extra-virgin olive oil** in a saucepan over medium heat until shimmering. Add **½ cup diced yellow onion** and cook until translucent, about 5 minutes. Add **1 tablespoon minced fresh ginger, 2 minced garlic cloves, 1 bay leaf, 1 teaspoon dried oregano, ½ teaspoon fenugreek seeds, ½ teaspoon turmeric, ¼ teaspoon ground cloves**, and **¼ teaspoon kosher salt**. Cook, stirring, for 3 minutes, then add **¼ cup diced red bell pepper** and **1 diced celery stalk**. Cook for a couple of minutes more.

Add **2 cups cauliflower florets, 1 cup diced zucchini, 2 tablespoons sugar**, and **¼ cup apple cider vinegar** and stir. Raise the heat to high, cook for a couple of minutes more, then cover, reduce the heat to low, and simmer until the vegetables are cooked through and the sauce has reduced, about 20 minutes. Add **½ cup thawed frozen peas** and cook, covered, for 5 more minutes. Taste and adjust the seasoning. Cool to room temperature and serve.

Makes 3½ cups. Store in the refrigerator for up to 4 days. Wouldn't kick **Dorset** (see page 87) out of bed. Delicious with fried eggs on toast, or over rice with a dollop of yogurt and chopped cilantro and scallion.

GREVENBROEKER
Notes of grape jelly, charcoal, and cayenne, with a fudgy, cobbled paste

Remember the taste of frozen grape juice concentrate? You'll find in in Grevenbroeker, an uber-fruity blue with a peppery finish. Grevenbrocker's curds are loosely packed by hand, allowing blue mold to flourish organically in the air pockets between curds, and resulting in an unusual-looking marbleized blue with an unmistakeable handmade touch.

ROASTED CONCORD GRAPES WITH THYME
You'll need Concord grapes, olive oil, lemon, red pepper flakes, fresh thyme

The concentrated grapiness of Concords is bold enough to handle the fruity intensity of Grevenbroeker. Chile and lemon bring heat and brightness to the grapes, while thyme lends a sweet herbaceousness. There's a slight oiliness to Concords, which plays nicely with the rich, dense butterfat of Grevenbroecker.

Preheat the oven to 425°F. In a glass baking dish, toss **1 cup Concord grapes** with **1 tablespoon olive oil, 1 teaspoon lemon zest, ¹⁄₈ teaspoon red pepper flakes, ¹⁄₈ teaspoon kosher salt**, and a **crack of black pepper**. And **4 sprigs of thyme** and roast until the grape skins split, about 15 minutes. Discard the thyme and cool for 5 minutes. Spoon the pan juices over the grapes when plating.

Makes enough for 4. Also yummy with **Kunik** (see page 32) and **Manchego** (see page 116).

DRINK ME
Chimay Triple Blanche
Trappist Ale, Baileux, Belgium
Medium-full body with notes of citrus, hops, and yeast

There's truth in the maxim "If it grows together, it goes together." Floral, fruity flavors start sweet and drift into a clean, dry finish that's a great match across the plate.

CHATELAIN
CAMEMBERT DE
NORMANDIE
Pasteurized Cow's Milk
Basse-Normandie, France

LO BRUSC ROSEMARY
HONEY

HAYSTACK
MOUNTAIN GOAT
DAIRY CAMEMBERT
Pasteurized Goat's Milk
Longmont, Colorado

CREAMED CORN &
PICKLED MUSTARD SEEDS

SWEET GRASS
DAIRY GREEN HILL
Pasteurized Cow's Milk
Thomasville, Georgia

CRACKLIN' JACK

CAMEMBARELY

Authentic French Camembert—
a soft-ripened cow's milk cheese
from Normandy—is served
alongside two American riffs
on the Camembert style: creamy
rounds of ooey-gooey glory in
a mushroom cloud of white mold.
Homespun accompaniments
add a lighthearted touch of
Americana to this homage to an
iconic French cheese.

CHATELAIN CAMEMBERT DE NORMANDIE
Notes of steamed cauliflower, warm milk and white truffle, with a rich, springy paste and white bloomy rind

Chatelain Camembert de Normandie is by far the most savory of the three cheeses, redolent of tree trunks after the rain.

The mellow sweetness of **Lo Brusc Rosemary Honey** has subtle woodland flavors that complement the meatiness of Camembert de Normandie. Delicious with so many mild, creamy cheeses, including **La Tur** (see page 106), **Selles-sur-Cher** (see page 74), and **Brie** (see pages 28 and 54).

SWEET GRASS DAIRY GREEN HILL
Notes of buttered popcorn and button mushroom, with a creamy paste and white bloomy rind

Sweet Grass Dairy's award-winning Green Hill captures the essence of Georgia sunshine, with a golden yellow paste full of grassy goodness. An approachable puck with a buoyant paste and balanced saltiness, it's a true Southern belle.

CRACKLIN' JACK
You'll need peanut oil, popcorn kernels, pork cracklings, dark brown sugar, honey, unsalted butter, vanilla extract, baking soda, redskin peanuts

You wouldn't want to eat an entire bowl of Cracklin' Jack, but a nip of crisp, caramel-clad pork rinds tossed with salty popcorn and peanuts beside a sexy wedge of Green Hill? Yes.

Preheat the oven to 250°F. Line a baking sheet with parchment paper.

In a large stockpot, pop **¼ cup popcorn kernels** in **2 tablespoons hot peanut oil**. Transfer to a large bowl and mix in **1 cup pork cracklings**.

In a small saucepan, cook **½ cup dark brown sugar**, **¼ cup honey**, and **3 tablespoons melted butter** over medium heat without stirring until it reaches 250°F on a candy thermometer, about 6 minutes. Remove from the heat and quickly stir in **1 teaspoon vanilla extract** and **½ teaspoon baking soda**. The mixture will bubble up, so work with caution.

Pour the hot sugar mixture over the popcorn and cracklings and stir with a heat-proof spatula. Fold in **¼ cup redskin peanuts**. Spread onto the prepared baking sheet and bake for 30 to 40 minutes, stirring every 10 minutes, until dry. Cool completely on the pan on a wire rack (the caramel will harden as the Jack cools).

Makes 5 cups. Store in an airtight container in a cool, dry place for up to 2 weeks. Show restraint. Delicious paired with **Irish Porter** (see page 155) and **Ossau Iraty Vieille** (see page 50). A decadent, fun bar snack for a cocktail party.

HAYSTACK MOUNTAIN GOAT DAIRY CAMEMBERT

Notes of wild onions and pickled mushrooms, with a creamy, runny paste and white bloomy rind

Haystack Mountain Goat Dairy Camembert is true to its French namesake, delivering on the hallmarks of the genre. Notes of spring onion add a savory complexity to the bright, tangy/herbal foundation of the cheese.

CREAMED CORN & PICKLED MUSTARD SEEDS

You'll need fresh corn, unsalted butter, shallot, sugar, heavy cream, yellow mustard seeds, white wine vinegar, bay leaf, dry mustard

Pickled mustard seeds add savory brightness to the sweetness of the creamed corn and the tang of Haystack Mountain Camembert.

For the creamed corn:
Bring a large pot of water to a boil. Add **2 ears of corn** and cook until tender, about 8 minutes. Drain and cool. With a sharp knife, cut the corn kernels from the cob into a shallow bowl. Into a separate bowl, scrape the back of a tablespoon down the cobs to extract the corn pulp and juices.

In a medium sauté pan, melt **1 tablespoon butter** over medium heat. Add **1 tablespoon diced shallot** and cook until translucent, 2 to 3 minutes. Add the corn kernels and **½ teaspoon sugar** and sauté for 2 minutes. Add **¼ cup heavy cream**, the corn pulp and juices, and a **pinch of kosher salt** and cook until the liquid has almost evaporated (you want this thick). Cool to room temperature before serving, but be sure to serve within the hour.

Makes 1 cup. Also a great match with **Brebirousse d'Argental** (see page 50).

For the pickled mustard seeds:
Rinse **1 cup yellow mustard seeds** in a fine-mesh sieve. In a small saucepan, combine the mustard seeds with **1 cup white wine vinegar** and let sit for 1 hour. Add **1 cup sugar, 1 bay leaf, ½ teaspoon dry mustard**, and ½ teaspoon red pepper flakes and bring to a boil. Reduce the heat to low and simmer until the mustard seeds are plump and tender, about 5 minutes. Remove and discard the bay leaf and transfer the pickled mustard seeds to a nonreactive airtight container. Refrigerate until ready to serve.

Makes 1 cup. Store in the refrigerator for up to 1 week. Tasty on its own with **Clothbound Cheddars** (see pages 137 to 138) and **Alpine cheeses** (see pages 102 to 103). So good slathered on hot buttered potatoes.

CAPRIOLE DAIRY
PIPER'S PYRAMID

Pasteurized Goat's Milk
Greenville, Indiana

ROASTED FIDDLEHEAD
FERNS WITH SWEET
PAPRIKA

CONSIDER
BARDWELL FARM
DORSET

Raw Cow's Milk
West Pawlet, Vermont

BUTTER-POACHED
MOREL MUSHROOMS

**MEADOWOOD FARMS
LEDYARD**

Pasteurized Sheep's Milk
Cazenovia, New York

PACIFIC PICKLE WORKS
ASPARAGUSTO!

SPRING, SPRUNG

Come spring, cheese makers are literally up to
their elbows in fresh milk. The season bursts with
new life: Baby animals romp on the grass while
their mothers bask in long-awaited sunshine.
Here, goat, cow, and sheep's milk cheeses sit side
by side; contrasting milks are an easy way to
vary flavors within a flight. Simple vegetable
accompaniments remind us that quality ingredients benefit most from restraint.

CAPRIOLE DAIRY PIPER'S PYRAMID

Notes of sweet paprika, lemon zest, and goat's milk yogurt with a light, cheesecakey paste and paprika-dusted, bloomy rind

Dense and moist, with a creamy, fluffy mouthfeel punctuated by a dusting of sweet paprika, Piper's Pyramid embodies the tangy, lemony flavors of expertly matured young goat cheese.

ROASTED FIDDLEHEAD FERNS WITH SWEET PAPRIKA

You'll need fiddlehead ferns, lemon, unsalted butter, sweet paprika

Blink and you could miss the annual harvest of fiddlehead ferns, which can last as few as two weeks. This spring delicacy is the young shoots of wild ferns, best prepared simply and with a gentle hand: Blanching and a light sauté are all that's needed. To extend the season a bit longer, fiddlehead ferns can be frozen after blanching. Place them between layers of parchment paper in a freezer container and freeze for up to 3 months.

Soak **12 fiddleheads** in cool water with the **juice of ½ lemon**. Agitate the water a bit so that any soil stuck to the ferns is released. Remove with a slotted spoon and drain on paper towels.

Bring water to a boil in a medium saucepan. Blanch the fiddleheads for 3 minutes. Remove with a slotted spoon and drain on paper towels.

In a medium sauté pan, melt **1 tablespoon butter** over medium heat until foaming. Add the fiddleheads and gently sauté for 3 to 4 minutes. Remove from the heat, spritz with the juice of **½ lemon**, and sprinkle with **½ teaspoon sweet paprika**. Season with salt. Serve immediately.

Also tasty paired with **Camembert de Normandie** (see page 82) and **Brebirousse d'Argental** (see page 50).

CONSIDER BARDWELL FARM DORSET

Notes of scrambled eggs, charcoal, and braised greens, with a smooth, firm paste and orange-hued washed rind

Dorset has an essentially meaty character, with earthy/nutty notes. Its texture is quite remarkable: so dense and rich it's like browned butter in solid form. Dorset turns creamier as it matures, but is also fantastic when young.

BUTTER-POACHED MOREL MUSHROOMS

You'll need morel mushrooms, unsalted butter, black peppercorns, bay leaf

Morels are little nuggets with deep, woodsy flavors—an earthy outlier to the lighter, fresher flavors associated with the season. They're excellent when poached in good butter and properly seasoned, shadowing the butter and soil umami of Dorset.

Brush **12 morel mushrooms** with a pastry brush to remove dirt and sediment. Trim off the woody, dry part of their stems.

Bring **½ cup water** to a simmer in a medium saucepan over medium-low heat. Whisk in **½ cup cold cubed butter**, one piece at a time, incorporating each piece before adding the next. Add **1 teaspoon black peppercorns**, **1 bay leaf**, and **½ teaspoon kosher salt** and gently poach the mushrooms until tender, 10 minutes or so. Remove with a slotted spoon and serve immediately.

Also yummy with **Pleasant Ridge Reserve Extra Aged** (see page 169).

MEADOWOOD FARMS LEDYARD

Notes of barnyard, Concord grapes, and yeast with a creamy, runny paste enrobed in grape leaves and washed in beer

This creamy, funky little jewel of sheepiness is washed in Empire Brewing Company Deep Purple, a local wheat beer infused with Concord grape juice, which imparts a fruity tone to the cheese. Ledyard's robust flavors and satiny texture howl for acidity, which **Pacific Pickle Works Asparagusto!** delivers in the tangy, vegetal snap of asparagus spears laced with just a touch of heat.

WRAPTURE

Unwrapping a puck of leaf-wrapped cheese feels special, a beautiful bespoke gift from Mother Nature. But leaves are more than eye-catching giftwrap: They keep cheese moist and can impart subtle earthy, woody, and vegetal notes. Three different styles of cheese—fresh, soft-ripened, and blue—demonstrate the adaptable charm of the genre.

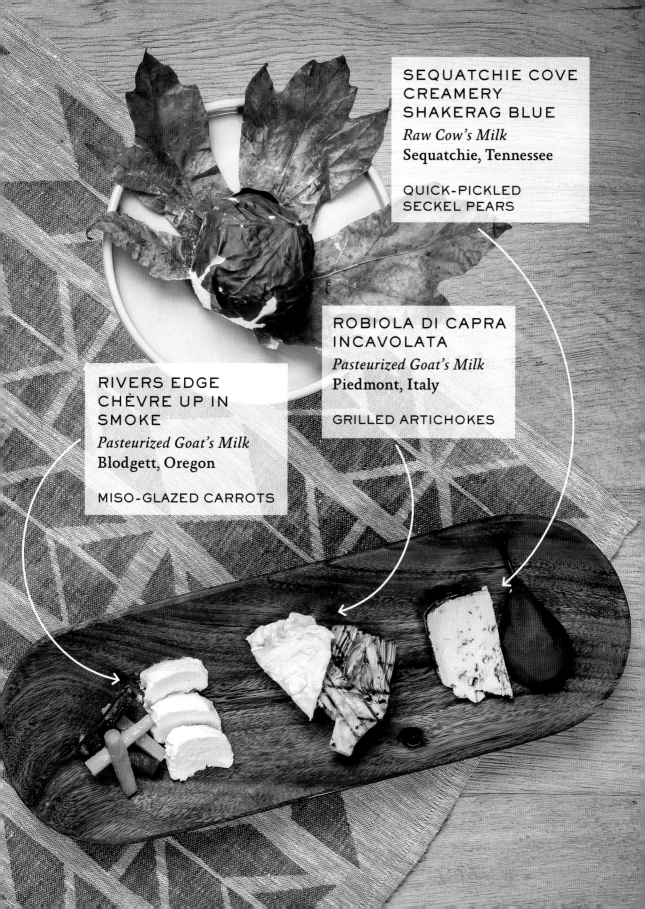

SEQUATCHIE COVE CREAMERY SHAKERAG BLUE
Raw Cow's Milk
Sequatchie, Tennessee

QUICK-PICKLED SECKEL PEARS

ROBIOLA DI CAPRA INCAVOLATA
Pasteurized Goat's Milk
Piedmont, Italy

GRILLED ARTICHOKES

RIVERS EDGE CHÈVRE UP IN SMOKE
Pasteurized Goat's Milk
Blodgett, Oregon

MISO-GLAZED CARROTS

RIVERS EDGE CHÈVRE UP IN SMOKE

Notes of preserved lemon and maple smoke, with a fresh, moist paste enrobed in smoked maple leaves

Up in Smoke is a slightly granular chèvre with three layers of smoke: Both the cheese and its maple leaf cloak are wood-smoked; a spritz of bourbon on the leaves lends its own smoky notes. A powerful citrusy tang saves this cheese from burnout.

MISO-GLAZED CARROTS

You'll need yellow miso paste, maple syrup, orange, nutmeg, white pepper, carrots, cumin seeds, unsalted butter

Miso marries with sweet carrots in an umami-fueled punch up against the intense smokiness of Up in Smoke. Toasted cumin seeds add texture and subtle warmth.

In a small bowl, whisk together **1 tablespoon yellow miso, 1 tablespoon maple syrup**, the **zest and juice of ½ orange**, **⅛ teaspoon freshly grated nutmeg**, and **⅛ teaspoon freshly ground white pepper**.

Cut **2 medium carrots** into 2 by ½-inch batons. In a medium sauté pan, toast **2 tablespoons cumin seeds** over medium heat until fragrant. Transfer to a small bowl. In the same pan, melt **2 tablespoons butter** over medium heat until foaming. Toss in the carrots and sauté until they begin to brown, 6 to 7 minutes. Pour the miso sauce over the carrots and cook until the sauce reduces, 3 to 4 minutes. Remove from the heat, garnish with the toasted cumin seeds, and serve.

Makes 1 cup. Also a great match with **Cabot Clothbound Cheddar** (see page 138) and **Gabietou** (see page 32).

ROBIOLA DI CAPRA INCAVOLATA

Notes of lemon peel and sautéed cabbage with a creamy, runny paste and Geotrichum rind enrobed in fresh cabbage leaves

Robiola di Capra Incavolata's humble, bright green cabbage leaf frock is a real stunner, imparting subtle earthy/vegetal tones that mellow the high-acid tang and yeasty flavors of this goat's milk puck. It's cheese meets stuffed cabbage.

GRILLED ARTICHOKES
You'll need marinated artichokes, olive oil

The smoky char and garlic-and-dried-herb brine of grilled marinated artichokes cut through Robiola di Capra Incavolata's richness.

Drain **4 large marinated artichokes** and pat dry with a paper towel. If whole, cut each in half.

Heat **1 tablespoon olive oil** in a cast-iron or nonstick grill pan over medium-high heat until almost smoking. Sear the artichokes, cut-side down, turning every 2 minutes. Since the artichokes are preserved, they don't need to be cooked much—aim for good-looking grill marks. Serve immediately.

Makes 8. Wouldn't kick **Sainte-Maure de Touraine** (see page 40) or **Ledyard** (see page 87) out of bed.

SEQUATCHIE COVE CREAMERY SHAKERAG BLUE
Notes of buttered crackers, root beer, and dried fig, with a firm, craggy paste enrobed in fig leaves

Shakerag Blue, a medium-bodied blue with a boozy fruitcake feel, wrapped in fig leaves soaked in local Tennessee whiskey.

QUICK-PICKLED SECKEL PEARS
You'll need Seckel (or small Anjou or Bartlett) pears, lemon, lime, rice vinegar, ruby port, sugar, honey, vanilla bean, cinnamon stick, whole cloves

Ruby port piques the dried fruit notes of Shakerag Blue, while the acidity and dark spices of the brine soothe its butterfat in this take on a classic pairing.

Peel and core **4 small Seckel pears**, leaving the stems intact. Place the prepared pears in a bowl with **2 cups water** and the **juice of ½ lemon**.

Peel **¼ lime** into thick strips with a vegetable peeler. In a small saucepan, combine **1 cup rice vinegar, 1 cup water, ½ cup ruby port, ½ cup sugar, ¼ cup honey, 1 split vanilla bean, 1 cinnamon stick, ½ teaspoon whole cloves**, and the lime peel and bring to a boil over high heat. Reduce the heat to low and simmer for 5 minutes.

Drain the pears and transfer to a 1-quart glass jar with a lid. Pour the hot liquid over the pears, covering them completely with liquid. Cool to room temperature, ball up some plastic wrap, and place on top of the pears to keep them submerged in the liquid. Tightly seal the lid and refrigerate for a minimum of 2 days.

Makes 4. Store in the refrigerator for up to 3 weeks. Delicious with **Valdeon** (see page 33) and **Tetilla** (see page 124).

HAZELNUT-PAPRIKA AND CHIVE BOURSIN CHEESE BALLS

PORT WINE CHEDDAR

PARTY LIKE IT'S 1979

Today's cheese options are so much better than they were decades ago, but that doesn't mean the cheesy tropes of yesteryear should disappear like the 8-track. More a reason to throw a retro cheese-themed party than a cheese plate per se, these kitschy, updated adaptations of groovy classics are a fun celebration that we've come a long way, baby.

ALPINE CHEESE
FONDUE

PORT WINE CHEDDAR

You'll need unsalted butter, shallot, ruby port, cheddar cheese, smooth Dijon mustard, lemon, mace, white pepper

Use real cheddar here, made from real milk, but don't break the bank. High-quality supermarket cheddar is fine (I use **Tillamook Medium Cheddar**). This throwback dip is best after the flavors have had a day or two to come together, so plan accordingly.

In a small sauté pan, melt **1 tablespoon butter** over medium-low heat. Add **1 minced shallot** and cook until soft and browned, about 4 minutes. Add **1 tablespoon ruby port** and cook until the liquid has been absorbed, about 3 minutes.

In a food processor, combine **1 pound shredded cheddar cheese, ½ cup ruby port, 2 tablespoons softened butter, 1 tablespoon smooth Dijon mustard, 1 teaspoon fresh lemon juice, ½ teaspoon ground mace,** and **¼ teaspoon freshly ground white pepper** and pulse until smooth. Add the onion-port mixture and process until fully incorporated.

Makes 2 cups. Store in the refrigerator for up to 2 weeks. Bring to room temperature before serving.

A port reduction drizzled over the port wine cheddar is a "little something extra" to add when serving on a particularly festive occasion. It isn't obligatory, but it adds pizzazz and a sweet, grapey touch. Tasty on its own with **Grevenbroecker** (see page 79), **Zimbro** (see page 132), or **Valdeon** (see page 33).

In a small saucepan, cook **1 cup ruby port** and **½ cup sugar** over medium-low heat until it coats a spoon and reduces to ¼ cup, about 30 minutes. Store in a tightly sealed nonreactive container in a cool, dark place for up to 1 month.

HAZELNUT-PAPRIKA AND CHIVE BOURSIN CHEESE BALLS

You'll need Boursin cheese, unsalted butter, chives, hazelnuts, sweet paprika

At one time or another we've all felt just a little bit fancy eating Boursin. And it's still good, in a nostalgic, processed cheese, guilty pleasure kind of way. Unlike all the other cheeses in this book, serve these balls chilled (but not right-out-of-the-refrigerator cold).

In a medium bowl, mix **2 packages Garlic & Fines Herbes–flavor Boursin cheese** and **2 tablespoons softened butter** with a wooden spoon. Roll into 12 balls, place on a plate lined with parchment paper, and chill for 2 or more hours. Can be prepared 1 day in advance.

Before serving, put **1 bunch finely chopped chives** in a wide-bottomed bowl. In a separate wide-bottomed bowl, combine **¼ cup finely chopped toasted hazelnuts** and **1 teaspoon sweet paprika**. Roll 6 of the chilled cheese balls in the chives and return them to the refrigerator. One at a time, wrap the remaining cheese balls in a small piece of paper towel, with the manufactured edge at its circumference. Dust the exposed cheese with the hazelnut-paprika mixture. Chill until ready to serve.

Makes 12.

ALPINE CHEESE FONDUE

You'll need Alpine cheese, cornstarch, garlic, dry white wine, cream cheese, nutmeg; toasted bread cubes, cornichons, apple slices for serving

Why suffer through a broken fondue? This fondue "cheat" may get me banned from Switzerland for life, but it works. The secret is cream cheese. Just a tad, I promise. Its stabilizers go a long way in preventing breakage, and don't compromise the overall flavor of the fondue.

Toss **2 pounds shredded Alpine cheese** (I used **1 pound Gruyère** and **1 pound Emmentaler**) with **1 tablespoon cornstarch**.

Rub **1 garlic clove** along the inside of a fondue pot or heavy-bottomed medium saucepan. Add **2 cups dry white wine** and bring to a simmer over medium-low heat. While whisking, add a small handful of the shredded cheese. Continue adding cheese one handful at a time, whisking continuously and adding more cheese only when the previous handful is fully incorporated. Whisk in **2 ounces softened cream cheese** and **½ teaspoon freshly grated nutmeg**. Serve immediately, in the warm pot, with plenty of toasted bread cubes, cornichons, and apple slices.

Serves 4 hungry guests.

RAM HALL DAIRY
BERKSWELL
Raw Sheep's Milk
West Midland, England

ENGLISH BREAKFAST
TEA JELLY

WESTCOMBE DAIRY
CAERPHILLY
Raw Cow's Milk
Somerset, England

QUICK-PICKLED
GOLDEN RAISINS

SHROPSHIRE BLUE
Pasteurized Cow's Milk
Leicestershire, England

TOASTED NORI
& HONEYCOMB

RULE, BRITANNIA

There's more to British cheese than Cheddar and Stilton. Contemporary British cheese makers are producing elegant, stalwart cheeses whose innovation lies in part in their nod to tradition. On the surface these cheeses have British reserve—you won't find them blustering for attention or making aggressive moves—but deep down they're quite punk rock: They are who they are, and make no apologies for it.

WESTCOMBE DAIRY CAERPHILLY
Notes of buttermilk, chive, and raw turnip with a dense, cakey paste and natural rind

Cheddar-like but not cheddar, with a beautiful specimen of a natural rind, Caerphilly is a curdy/buttery/tangy workingman's cheese, matured for four to six months. It's an easygoing, approachable choice when looking to cautiously expand your British cheese horizons.

QUICK-PICKLED GOLDEN RAISINS
You'll need yellow mustard seeds, honey, apple cider vinegar, golden raisins, bay leaf, cinnamon stick, fresh rosemary

Pickled golden raisins burst in the mouth, releasing sweet, tangy juices that penetrate the rich, sharp, compact paste of Caerphilly. Little pops of mustard seed add textural dimension.

In a small saucepan, toast **1 tablespoon yellow mustard seeds** over medium heat until they pop, then add **½ cup water**, **2 tablespoons honey**, **3 tablespoons apple cider vinegar**, **1 cup golden raisins**, **1 bay leaf**, **1 cinnamon stick**, **1 sprig rosemary**, and **½ teaspoon kosher salt** and bring to a boil. Reduce the heat to low and simmer until the mustard seeds are tender, the raisins are plump, and most of the liquid has evaporated, about 10 minutes. Remove and discard the bay leaf and cinnamon stick. Serve at room temperature or slightly chilled.

Makes 1 cup. Store in the refrigerator for up to 3 days. Also delicious with **Tetilla** (see page 124) and **Ossau Iraty Vieille** (see page 50). Fabulous tossed in an arugula salad or with couscous.

RAM HALL DAIRY BERKSWELL
Notes of dried apricot, tobacco, and mutton chop, with a firm, smooth paste and natural rind

The sheepy, toasted flavors of Berkswell bring to mind wool socks and warm tea, toasted biscuits and clotted cream. Berkswell is matured for six months; its smooth paste and fruity/nutty flavors are indicative of this classic style of aged sheep's milk cheese.

ENGLISH BREAKFAST TEA JELLY

You'll need English Breakfast loose-leaf tea, low-/no-sugar pectin, dark brown sugar, lemon

A take on biscuits and tea: The toasty, caramelized flavors of Berkswell are juxtaposed with the sweet comfort of tea jelly. Much like wine, black tea has a fair amount of tannins, a plant-based compound that adds astringent notes and flavor complexity. Tannins are what make flavors "dry," causing the palate to crave some soothing butterfat.

Bring **1 cup water** to a boil in a small saucepan. Turn off the heat and add **1 tablespoon loose-leaf English Breakfast tea**. Steep for 10 minutes. Strain the tea and return it to the saucepan.

Add **1 tablespoon low-/no-sugar pectin** and bring to a boil over medium-high heat, whisking frequently. Add **2 tablespoons dark brown sugar** and **¼ teaspoon fresh lemon juice**, raise the heat to high, and boil hard for another minute—the mixture will thicken. Remove from the heat, pour the hot jelly into two ¼-pint glass jars or one ½-pint glass jar, and cool to room temperature. The jelly will reach proper consistency as it cools. Tightly seal the jars and refrigerate until ready to serve.

Makes ½ pint. Store in the refrigerator for up to 1 month. Sidles up nicely to **Sainte-Maure de Touraine** (see page 40). Also a lovely host gift.

SHROPSHIRE BLUE

Notes of peanut butter, roasted radish, and tin, with a firm, mottled paste and natural rind

The visual charm of annatto coloring strikes again with Shropshire Blue, a traffic-cone-orange cheese with striated blue-green mold. Shropshire is relatively mild for its type, with distinctive nutty/metallic notes and a rich, dense paste.

Shropshire Blue's visage almost overwhelms its flavor; based on its appearance you might expect a bolder cheese, when in fact Shropshire is quite mellow. Sheets of **toasted nori seaweed** add crunch and salt to the pairing, drawing out the saline minerality of the cheese. **Honeycomb** soothes the saltiness and offers its own textural enhancement, in addition to sweet, earthy notes. The three elements of the pairing are meant to be eaten as one bite, like a sushi hand roll.

THE HILLS ARE ALIVE

Traditionally, Alpine cheeses are made during summer, when herds graze on wild mountain grasses, flowers, and herbs, producing flavorful, grassy/herbaceous milk. Cooked nutty and caramelized flavors abound in this style, which despite creeping modernity maintains its relationship to tradition and terroir.

**MARCEL PETITE
FORT ST. ANTOINE
COMTÉ**

Raw Cow's Milk
Franche-Comte, Jura, France

ANARCHY IN A JAR
BEER MUSTARD
& HUSK CHERRIES

**ROLF BEELER
GRUYÈRE**

Raw Cow's Milk
Fribourg, Switzerland

SUNFLOWER
SEED BRITTLE

ADELEGGER
Raw Cow's Milk, Allgau
Bavaria, Germany

FRIED ONION STRINGS

MARCEL PETITE FORT ST. ANTOINE COMTÉ

Notes of wildflowers, creamed nuts, and white grape juice, with a smooth, firm paste and natural rind

Comté is a benchmark French Alpine cheese, one of the most popular in France. It's widely available in the United States, from producers of varying quality levels. Marcel Petite Fort St. Antoine Comté is one of the most authentic and flavorful examples of this nutty/fruity/grassy icon.

Anarchy in a Jar Beer Mustard is a satisfying, pop-in-your-mouth "vegan caviar" (as the company cheekily bills it). Plump, juicy pearls of mustard carry a complex malty flavor with sweet, sour, and piquant notes that draw out the more savory aspects of Comté. Also delicious with **Caerphilly** (see page 98) and **Grayson** (see page 107).

Husk cherries (also known as ground cherries) look like gooseberries or small yellow cherry tomatoes in a golden husk (think tomatillos but small and sweet). Their flavor is a combination of persimmon, tomato, and pineapple notes. Don't discard the husk—it looks great on a cheese plate, though it shouldn't be eaten.

ROLF BEELER GRUYÈRE

Notes of bone marrow and onion rings, with a smooth, firm paste and natural rind

Thankfully, "Swiss cheese" no longer denotes bland, hole-y cheeses that look, feel, and taste like plastic. Gruyère is by far the most celebrated of the many fine Alpine cheeses of Switzerland, popular for its nutty, sweet, and savory notes. *Affineur* Rolf Beeler's Gruyère sees about twelve months of maturation before release.

SUNFLOWER SEED BRITTLE
You'll need sugar, light corn syrup, unsalted butter, baking soda, roasted sunflower seeds

Sunflower seed brittle does that sweet, salty, crunchy mash-up so well, and it reinforces the nutty/grassy/floral flavor redolent in Alpine cheese. Sunflower seeds harness the allusion to the sun, which fuels the grass, which makes the milk, which forms the cheese.

Line a large baking sheet with ½-inch sides with lightly oiled parchment paper and set aside.

In a large, heavy-bottomed saucepan, combine **1 cup sugar, ½ cup light corn syrup**, and **½ cup water** and cook over medium heat until the mixture turns light brown and reaches 320°F on a candy thermometer. Remove from the heat and mix in **1½ tablespoons butter, 1 teaspoon kosher salt**, and **½ teaspoon baking soda** with an oiled, heatproof spatula—proceed with caution, as the mixture will bubble and expand. Stir in **1½ cups roasted hulled sunflower seeds**, then carefully spread the hot brittle over the prepared baking sheet. Place a piece of parchment paper over the hot brittle and with a rolling pin roll it into a ½-inch-thick slab.

Cool completely on the baking sheet on a wire rack. Break into shards before serving.

Makes 1 pound. Store layered between parchment paper in an airtight container in a cool, dry place for up to 1 month. Tasty with **Ardrahan** (see page 158), **Gouda "Signature"** (see page 111), and **Berkswell** (see page 98).

ADELEGGER
Notes of beef broth and caramelized onions, with a firm paste and washed/natural rind

Washed in herb-infused white wine during its initial weeks, then aged for 18 months, Adelegger has the flaky texture of a Butterfinger candy bar. Powerful, savory flavors bloom in this fine example of traditional *Alpage* cheese making. Like a Philly cheesesteak, but just cheese.

FRIED ONION STRINGS
You'll need high-heat frying oil such as canola, grapeseed, or peanut oil, rice flour, yellow onion

The secret to perfect onion strings is frying them at the right temperature, in small batches, and retrieving them from the oil just as they start to color. Follow this advice, and you're golden (and crispy and delicious).

In a small saucepan, heat **1½ cups oil** over medium heat to 300°F degrees.

Meanwhile, put **½ cup rice flour** in a shallow bowl. Dredge **½ onion**, thinly sliced in the flour. When the oil comes to temperature, shake off excess flour and carefully drop the onion slices into the oil in three batches. When the onions begin to color, after 5 to 6 minutes, transfer to paper towels with a slotted spoon to drain. Residual heat will continue to cook them and they will turn the perfect shade of brown and be nice and crispy. Very lightly season with kosher salt—the Adelegger provides most of the salt in this pairing.

Makes ½ cup. Also a great match with **Red Hawk** (see page 158) and **Red Rock** (see page 179).

LANGRES

Pasteurized Cow's Milk
Ardenne, France

SPARKLING APPLE
CIDER JELLY

LA TUR

*Pasteurized Cow, Sheep,
and Goat's Milk*
Piedmont, Italy

CRISPY PROSCIUTTO
& DRIED CANTALOUPE

MEADOW CREEK
DAIRY GRAYSON
Raw Cow's Milk
Galax, Virginia

DEVILED LEMON CURD

SMOOTH MOVES
The seductive cheeses on this Barry White of flights are all about smooth, velvety creaminess. Like any good love song, each has just a whisper of funk to keep things interesting. The accompaniments' playful sweetness and tease of heat are a welcome tickle and nibble.

LA TUR

Notes of honeycomb, ripe melon, and moss, with a fluffy, ultra-creamy paste and wrinkled Geotrichum rind

The triple-milk threat of La Tur is key to its luscious, bright character; its three milks are harnessed to great effect. The brightness of goat's milk; the round rich, grassy flavors of cow's milk; and the unctuous butterfat of sheep's milk marry in a tangy, sweet cream bomb.

CRISPY PROSCIUTTO & DRIED CANTALOUPE

You'll need prosciutto, dried cantaloupe

All the notes needed for a "must keep eating" experience are here: The salty, fatty ham needs the sweet, earthy melon, and the melon needs the meaty tang of the prosciutto. Both lap up the sensual cream of La Tur. Good dried cantaloupe can be purchased at specialty markets and grocers.

Preheat the oven to 350°F. Place a wire rack on a baking sheet lined with parchment paper. Lay **4 slices prosciutto** on the rack, leaving ample space between each slice. Bake for about 10 minutes, until crisp. Cool completely and store layered between paper towels in an airtight container until ready to serve. Prosciutto chips are delicate—to prevent breakage, give them plenty of space.

Serve one piece each alongside a wedge of La Tur.

Makes 4. Store the prosciutto in a cool, dry place at room temperature for up to 3 days. A great match with **Clothbound Cheddars** (see pages 137 to 138), **Mahon** (see page 116), and **Grayson** (see page 107).

LANGRES

Notes of sweet cream, buttered toast, and cabbage, with a cakey, creamy paste and wrinkled, orange-hued washed/Geotrichum rind

Langres has yeasty, buttery, brioche-like notes and a faint aroma of wet mushroom. Topping off this stunner with some bubbly is a fabulous idea, as Langres's richness could use the lift, pop, and pep of bubbles.

SPARKLING APPLE CIDER JELLY
You'll need sparkling apple cider, low-/no-sugar pectin, cinnamon stick, sugar, vanilla bean

You could use Champagne as a nod to tradition, but sparkling cider is a more lighthearted ingredient enlivening the cheese with mouth-watering tartness.

In a medium saucepan, sprinkle **2 cups high-quality sparkling apple cider** (I used **Foggy Ridge Cider "Serious Cider"**) with **2 tablespoons low-/no-sugar pectin** and whisk to combine. Add **1 cinnamon stick** and bring to a boil over medium-high heat, whisking frequently. Add **¼ cup sugar**, raise the heat to high, and boil hard for another minute—the mixture will thicken. Remove from the heat and stir in the **seeds from 1 vanilla bean**. Pour the hot jelly into two ½-pint glass jars and cool to room temperature. Tightly seal the jars and store in the refrigerator until ready to serve.

Makes 1 pint. Store in the refrigerate for up to 1 month. Excellent with **Sainte-Maure de Touraine** (see page 40) and **Plain Young Gouda** (see page 110). Also a lovely host gift.

MEADOW CREEK DAIRY GRAYSON
Notes of fried egg, mustard flower, and dry-aged steak, with a supple paste and orange-hued washed rind

Grayson is *terroir* driven, with plenty of meaty/earthy/funky flavors. A silken sophisticate with a deep golden paste born of rich grazing grass, it has an addictive steak-and-eggs vibe.

DEVILED LEMON CURD
You'll need egg yolks, sugar, lemon, unsalted butter, cayenne pepper, sweet paprika, dried mustard

Grayson relishes the fresh lemon tang, and the "deviled" spices add BBQ notes to its meaty undertones.

In the top of a double boiler, whisk together **5 egg yolks**, **1 teaspoon sugar**, and **¼ cup fresh lemon juice**. Cook, whisking continuously, until the yolks thicken and their color lightens, 2 to 3 minutes. Work quickly—you don't want to end up with scrambled eggs.

Remove from the heat and whisk in **2 tablespoons room temperature cubed butter**, one cube at time. Add **⅛ teaspoon cayenne pepper**, **⅛ teaspoon sweet paprika**, **½ teaspoon dried mustard**, a **pinch of kosher salt**. Whisk to combine thoroughly. Refrigerate until slightly chilled, about 4 hours.

Makes 1 cup. Store in the refrigerator for up to 1 week. A nice match with **Red Hawk** (see page 158).

HOLLAND'S FAMILY CHEESE MARIEKE PLAIN YOUNG GOUDA

Raw Cow's Milk
Thorp, Wisconsin

APPLE CHUTNEY

L'AMUSE GOUDA "SIGNATURE"

Pasteurized Cow's Milk
Beemster, The Netherlands

AJVAR

L'AMUSE GOUDA "PRIL"

Pasteurized Cow's Milk
Beemster, The Netherlands

COFFEE-HAZELNUT CRISPS

AGING GRACEFULLY

There's a difference between aging and getting old: Cheeses matured under the skilled care of affineurs age; cheeses hanging out in a refrigerator get old. Three expertly matured Goudas—with a couple of months to a couple of years of maturation—demonstrate the perks of expert maintenance. Low-key accompaniments highlight the flavors and textures that bloom with age.

HOLLAND'S FAMILY CHEESE MARIEKE PLAIN YOUNG GOUDA

matured 2 to 4 months

Notes of fresh milk and honey, with a smooth, semi-firm paste and waxed rind

Marieke Plain Young Gouda is a snackable cheese that's tangy, clean, and mellow, with herbal/honey notes and a supple paste as smooth as a baby's butt. Its well-crafted youth is a sage entry point for exploring Gouda and Gouda-style cheeses.

APPLE CHUTNEY

You'll need unsalted butter, yellow onion, bay leaf, fresh ginger, Worcestershire sauce, apple, apple cider vinegar, orange, honey, celery seed, cumin, allspice

Apples and young Gouda are a classic combination—the sweet, tart fruit handles the tangy talkback of youthful cheese with aplomb. Cumin, allspice, celery seed, and Worcestershire add a savory, smoky layer to this sweet and tart chutney. Like a savory mulled apple cider.

In a medium saucepan, melt **1 tablespoon butter** over medium heat until foaming. Add **½ cup diced yellow onion** and **1 bay leaf** and cook until the onion is translucent and just starting to brown at the edges. Add **1 tablespoon minced fresh ginger** and **1 tablespoon Worcestershire sauce** and cook until the onion and ginger absorb the liquid, about 2 minutes.

Stir in **1 diced peeled medium-tart apple**, **¼ cup apple cider vinegar**, **½ teaspoon orange zest**, **¼ cup fresh orange juice**, **1 tablespoon honey**, **¼ teaspoon celery seed**, **¼ teaspoon cumin**, **¼ teaspoon kosher salt**, and **⅛ teaspoon ground allspice**. Raise the heat to high, bring to a boil, then reduce the heat to low and simmer, uncovered, stirring occasionally, until most of the liquid has evaporated, about 30 minutes. Remove and discard the bay leaf, cool to room temperature, and serve.

Makes 1½ cups. Store in an airtight container in the refrigerator for up to 3 days. Sidles up nicely to **Caerphilly** (see page 98). Also fantastic with Plain Young Gouda in a grilled cheese.

L'AMUSE GOUDA "PRIL"

matured 6 to 9 months

Notes of butterscotch, minerals, and soil, with a firm, crystalline paste and waxed rind

L'Amuse Gouda "Pril" is an example of how skilled maturation deepens and transforms cheese from something pleasant into something obsession-worthy. Foundational milky/grassy flavors are still there, but as a platform for emerging butterscotch and toffee notes.

COFFEE-HAZELNUT CRISPS

You'll need espresso, unsalted butter, honey, hazelnuts, flour

Nutty, coffee notes in the "Pril" reinforce similar flavors in this crisp. Hazelnuts mirror the creamy mouthfeel of the cheese.

Preheat the oven to 300°F. Line a baking sheet with parchment paper.

In a small bowl, combine **2 tablespoons brewed espresso, 2 tablespoons melted butter, 2 tablespoons honey, 2 tablespoons ground hazelnuts, 2 tablespoons all-purpose flour**, and **¼ teaspoon kosher salt**. Mix thoroughly and chill for 1 hour.

Drop ½-tablespoon mounds of batter 3 inches apart on the prepared baking sheet. Bake for about 12 minutes, until the edges of the crisps are quite dark. Cool on the pan for a minute or two, then transfer to a wire rack to cool completely.

Makes 18. Store between layers of parchment paper in an airtight container in a cool, dry place for up to 4 days. Wouldn't kick **Barely Buzzed** (see page 154) or **Bianco Sardo** (see page 151) out of bed.

L'AMUSE GOUDA "SIGNATURE"

matured 24 months

Notes of coffee, port wine, and Tabasco, with a hard, crystalline paste and waxed rind

L'Amuse Gouda "Signature" has that crunchy, crystalline paste coveted in aged Goudas—so mineral, it's like eating a cheesy stalactite. Beyond the crave-worthy texture, layers of vegetal/umami flavors abound, with bell pepper, black pepper, and burnt sugar notes. A Gouda for grown-ups.

Often referred to as the "caviar" of the Balkans, *ajvar* is a traditional Slavic condiment made primarily of roasted red peppers. Its sweet, smoky, bright undertones and fair amount of tannins draw out the earthy/vegetal flavors of the "signature." A chunky but spreadable puree is a welcome contrast to the toothsome cheese. Also yummy with **Piper's Pyramid** (see page 86) and **Mahon** (see page 116).

SPANISH STYLE

Spanish *quesos* have a sophisticated, chic rusticity that's both ancient and modern. Call it a Spanish paradox: Even cheeses lacking in traditional provenance have an elegant soulfulness that relishes vibrant accompaniments. Share with timeless beauties and hip icons.

LEONORA

Raw Goat's Milk
Castilla y León, Spain

POPPY SEED
CAVIAR & DRAGON
FRUIT CHIPS

MAHON
Raw Cow and Sheep's Milk
Minorca, Spain

GOYA GUAVA PASTE

LA OVEJA NEGRA ORGANIC MANCHEGO
Pasteurized Sheep's Milk
La Mancha, Spain

SWEET POTATO BUTTER & FRIED SAGE

LEONORA

Notes of lemon yogurt and chicken broth with a dense, flaky paste and white bloomy rind

Despite its stick-to-the-roof-of-your-mouth density, Leonora still pulls off the illusion of lightness—a testament to the magical acidity of goat's milk. True to type, Leonora has plenty of robust goaty/nutty notes, finishing with a spiced citrus note like a rich lemon-pepper sauce.

POPPY SEED CAVIAR & DRAGON FRUIT CHIPS

You'll need poppy seeds, condensed milk, lemon, vanilla extract, dragon fruit, sugar

Seeds add a wonderful textural component to cheese pairings, and poppy seeds in particular highlight the nutty/earthy notes of Leonora. Take a whiff of the poppy seeds when you drain them—they're like soil after a heavy rain.

For the poppy seed caviar:

In a small saucepan, combine **1½ cups water** and **½ cup poppy seeds** and bring to a simmer over medium heat. Cook for 15 minutes, then remove from the heat, cover, and let sit for 15 minutes. Repeat the process a second time. Drain in a very fine–mesh sieve, return the poppy seeds to the pan, add **½ cup condensed milk**, **1 strip of lemon peel**, and a **pinch of kosher salt**, and bring to a boil. Reduce the heat to low and simmer until the milk has evaporated and the mixture resembles a paste, about 15 minutes. Remove from the heat, remove and discard the lemon peel, and add **½ teaspoon vanilla extract**. Serve at room temperature.

Makes ¾ cup. Store in an airtight container in the refrigerator for up to 1 month. Tasty paired with **Pecorino Foglie di Noce** (see page 162).

For the dragon fruit chips:

Chill one **dragon fruit** in the refrigerator for a couple of hours. Preheat the oven to 250°F. Line a baking sheet with parchment paper.

Trim the scales off the dragon fruit, then halve crosswise and using a mandoline slice 4 (¹⁄₈-inch-thick) slices. In a small saucepan, simmer **¼ cup sugar** and **¼ cup water** over medium heat until the sugar dissolves. Remove from the heat and dredge the dragon fruit slices in the syrup. Place the slices on the prepared baking sheet and bake for 1 hour, turning the slices halfway through, until the chips are dry, crisp, and beginning to color.

Store between layers of parchment in an airtight container in a cool, dry place for up to 3 days.

MAHON
Notes of olives and stewed plums, with a firm, cakey paste and natural rind

Preserved flavors abound in Mahon, a briny, pickle-y, salt-cured strut. When young, Mahon has fruity/floral notes; with maturity, it takes a flaky turn and salted fruit-and-vegetable flavors emerge. Think umeboshi plum.

Mahon is an opportunity to put ubiquitous supermarket *dulce* **Goya Guava Paste** to good use. The guava paste's citrusy sweet-and-sour flavors meld with Mahon in a pairing that's salty, sweet, and sticky. Also tasty with **Fat Bottom Girl** (see page 125) and **Berkswell** (see page 98).

LA OVEJA NEGRA ORGANIC MANCHEGO
Notes of lemon, hay, and cinnamon toast, with a firm, crumbly paste and natural rind

Made from the milk of rare black Manchega sheep, La Oveja Negra has all the hallmarks of a finely crafted Manchego: Sheepy/barnyard notes intersperse with grassy/hay flavors with a dulce de leche sweetness.

SWEET POTATO BUTTER & FRIED SAGE
You'll need sweet potatoes, fresh ginger, unsalted butter, sherry vinegar, maple syrup, cumin, cinnamon, nutmeg, olive oil, sage

Manchego's dry, crumbly paste calls for a high-moisture accompaniment, and Sweet Potato Butter delivers. The sweet acidity of sherry vinegar brightens the butter and the cheese, while fresh ginger lends subtle heat, and cumin and cinnamon whisper of smoke and wood. Like a sweet potato pie filling with attitude.

For the sweet potato butter:
Preheat the oven to 400°F. Line a baking sheet with parchment paper. Prick **2 medium sweet potatoes** with a fork and roast on the baking sheet until soft, about 45 minutes. When the potatoes are cool enough to handle, peel and process the flesh in a food processor until smooth.

Cut **1 (2-inch) piece fresh peeled ginger** into 4 or 5 discs and transfer to a small saucepan. Add **3 tablespoons butter** and cook over medium heat until the butter just starts to brown. Whisk in **1 tablespoon sherry vinegar, 1 teaspoon maple syrup, ¹⁄₈ teaspoon ground cumin, ¹⁄₈ teaspoon ground cinnamon, and ¹⁄₈ teaspoon freshly grated nutmeg** and cook for another minute. Remove from the heat, add to the food processor with the sweet potato, and pulse until completely incorporated. Season to taste with salt and pepper. Serve at room temperature.

Makes 1 cup. Store in an airtight container in the refrigerator for up to 4 days. Also a great match with **Serpa** (see page 133) and **Gabietou** (see page 32).

For the fried sage:
In a small sauté pan, heat **3 tablespoons olive oil** until fragrant and shimmering. Fry **4 sage leaves** until curled and crisp. Drain on a paper towel. Serve immediately.

DRINK ME
Both dry and sweet styles of sherry are a natural pairing with cheese—especially Spanish cheese.

El Maestro Sierra Oloroso 15 Anõs
Oloroso & Pedro Jimenez grapes, Jerez, Spain
Full bodied and dry, with notes of hazelnut, figs, and mulling spices

A mellow, nutty, dry sherry with herbal brightness friendly to the entire flight.

Lustau East India Solera Reserva
Oloroso & Pedro Jimenez grapes, Jerez, Spain
Full bodied and sweet with notes of toasted cashews, orange peel, cardamom, and raisins

A clean, complex, sweet sherry managing lightness amid deep cacao and toffee notes. Drinks especially well with the Mahon and Sweet Potato Butter.

RUSH CREEK WEEKEND

Rush Creek Reserve is a creamy cold-weather treat made from the milk of cows who've transitioned from eating (summer) pasture to (winter) hay. This dietary disruption impacts milk composition and makes a rich, custardy spoon cheese that's pure decadence. Drizzled on crisp tempura and griddled greens and slathered on crusty bread, it's a sophisticated communal meal.

UPLANDS CHEESE
COMPANY RUSH
CREEK RESERVE

Raw Cow's Milk
Dodgeville, Wisconsin

TEMPURA
WATERCRESS

CAST-IRON
ENDIVES

TEMPURA
OLIVES

UPLANDS CHEESE COMPANY RUSH CREEK RESERVE
Notes of beef broth and spruce, with a silken paste and washed rind trussed in spruce bark

Rush Creek Reserve is inspired by a traditional French and Swiss winter Alpine cheese, Vacherin Mont d'Or. It's made from the winter milk of cows; during the summer, the same cows produce the milk for **Pleasant Ridge Reserve** (see page 169). A creamy stew of über-rich butterfat is laced with beef and woodland flavors tucked beneath a furry white rind. It's an impossible cheese to "cut": Rush Creek is a spoon cheese all the way.

If you're planning on replicating this cheese presentation to a T, make the accompaniments in the order written.

CAST-IRON ENDIVES
You'll need Belgian endives, sherry vinegar, extra-virgin olive oil, high-heat neutral oil such as canola or grapeseed oil

Belgian endives are quite bitter—a vegetal counterpoint to Rush Creek's meaty cream. Sherry vinegar helps the endives caramelize during grilling and adds zing. Also delicious with tangy, creamy cheeses like **La Tur** (see page 106) and **Robiola di Capra Incavolata** (see page 90) and moist blue cheeses like **Roquefort** (see page 29), **Valdeon** (see page 33), and **Smokey Blue** (see page 146).

Heat a large cast-iron pan (if you have a cast-iron grill pan, even better) over medium-high heat until very hot and almost smoking.

Quarter **4 Belgian endives** lengthwise. Whisk together **1 tablespoon sherry vinegar**, **2 tablespoons extra-virgin olive oil**, **a pinch of kosher salt**, and freshly **ground black pepper** to taste in a small bowl.

Add enough **high-heat oil** to lightly coat the pan. Brush the endives with the dressing, reserving the remaining dressing. Cook, turning once, until tender and charred, about 15 minutes. Serve at room temperature, drizzled with the remaining dressing.

TEMPURA WATERCRESS & OLIVES
You'll need high-heat frying oil such as canola, grapeseed, or peanut, watercress, egg yolks, cake flour, cornstarch, lemon, dry-cured black olives

Like Belgian endive, watercress is an assertive, bitter green, though heartier than endive and with a peppery bite. The double-whammy richness of Rush Creek paired with tempura is admittedly excessive, but the tempura's crisp texture contrasts the creamy cheese, and the bitter tones of watercress and lemon rein in the richness. Dry-cured black olives are little bullets of concentrated, salty umami flavor.

In a heavy-bottomed pot with high sides, heat **2 cups oil** over medium heat to 350°F. Meanwhile, prepare the cheese, vegetables, and tempura batter.

Preheat the oven to 250°F. Clean and thoroughly dry **1 large bunch watercress**.

Wrap a room-temperature Rush Creek Reserve in aluminum foil. Bake for about 15 minutes, until the cheese is molten. It should be ready to eat at about the same time as the tempura.

In a medium bowl, combine **1 cup water** and **1 cup ice**, then divide into 1 cup chilled water and ¼ cup ice cubes.

Place **2 egg yolks** in a large bowl. Add **½ cup cake flour**, **½ cup cornstarch**, the chilled water, and the ice cubes and mix lightly with chopsticks. Don't overmix; it's okay if some pockets of dry flour remain.

Spread **½ cup cake flour** on a baking sheet and line a second baking sheet with paper towels. Position the bowl of batter near the hot oil.

Toss one-quarter of the watercress in the cake flour, making sure the flour sticks to the watercress. Shake off excess flour, toss through the batter to coat, and place in the hot oil. Drizzle a bit of batter on top of the frying watercress using chopsticks—this will help achieve the crispy, lacy tempura. Fry until the bottom of the watercress is golden, about 2 minutes, then turn with chopsticks or a slotted spoon and fry for another minute or two. Transfer to the paper towel–lined baking sheet, spritz with **lemon juice**, and season very, very lightly with kosher salt. Fry the remaining watercress in three batches.

Add **½ cup pitted oil-cured black olives** to the remaining batter and fry two or three at a time (the olives may cluster together, which is fine), turning with a slotted spoon, until the batter is golden, 1 to 2 minutes. Transfer to the paper towel–lined baking sheet. Serve both tempuras immediately.

DRINK ME

Foggy Ridge Cider "Serious Cider"

English and American heirloom apples, Dogspur, Virginia

Full body, with notes of lime zest, wet stone, and peach

Bright acidity and a crisp finish make this dry, English-style hard cider a punchy, punctuating match for the velvety tones of Rush Creek Reserve.

ANATOMY 101

Here lies a cheeky cheese plate that's a nod to the whimsical tradition of anatomically themed cheeses. Share with pun-loving guests who'll appreciate a slightly ribald selection of robust cheeses and accompaniments.

TETILLA
Pasteurized Cow's Milk
Galicia, Spain

LAVENDER-QUINCE
PASTE

**BLEATING HEART
CHEESE FAT
BOTTOM GIRL**
Raw Sheep's Milk
Tomales, California

BLACK & WHITE
SESAME CRISPS

TÊTE DE MOINE
Raw Cow's Milk
Jura, Switzerland

FARMHOUSE CULTURE
SPICY WAKAME
GINGER KIMCHI

TÊTE DE MOINE

Notes of mustard and French onion soup, with a firm, moist paste and natural/washed rind

The monks who invented tangy/funky/fruity Tête de Moine eight centuries ago clearly had a sense of humor: *tête de moine* is French for "monk's head," a reference to the size and shape of the cheese, and to the *girolle*—a slicer that "shaves" the cheese into thin curls, exposing a cheesy bald spot resembling the monks' iconic hairstyle.

If you don't have a *girolle* (and most likely, you don't), slice the top of the rind and use a sharp paring knife or vegetable peeler to shave paper-thin curls of Tête de Moine. It's worth the effort: It looks great on the plate and releases the concentrated flavors of the cheese.

Tête de Moine robustness requires a pairing with acidity and depth, which **Farmhouse Culture Spicy Wakame Ginger Kimchi** succinctly delivers. Their organic kimchi is a layered, not-too-spicy raw fermentation of cabbage, carrots, radish, ginger, and wakame seaweed. The ginger and carrot are of particular note in this pairing: Fruity/vegetal notes highlight similar notes in the Tête de Moine. A fun match with **Gabietou** (see page 32) and **Red Hawk** (see page 158).

TETILLA

Notes of marshmallow crème, papaya, and vanilla bean, with a silky, semi-firm paste and waxed rind

The literal translation of *tetilla* is "nipple," an apt name because of the cheese's voluptuous shape and unabashed milky-ness. Tetilla is as supple as a skilled gymnast—smooth and nimble, with graceful fluidity and sweet, tangy moves. Avoid Tetilla's rind—it's not meant for eating.

LAVENDER-QUINCE PASTE
You'll need quince, unsalted butter, sugar, lemon, culinary-grade lavender essential oil

Quince paste (*membrillo* in Spanish) is a popular cheese accompaniment. Its sticky, compact texture and sweet/tart flavors pair with many cheeses. A touch of lavender harnesses the tart fruit's floral underpinnings. Quince also lets you know when it's done cooking, turning a beautiful shade of dusky pink. Tetilla's lactic trill is a great canvas for the sweet, tart, floral notes of quince.

Preheat the oven to 350°F.

Rinse and dry **2 pounds (about 3 large) quinces**, place them in a buttered 8 x 8-inch baking dish, tightly cover the pan with aluminum foil, and bake until the quince are tender, about 1 hour.

When cool enough to handle, peel, core, and seed the quince. Process in a food processor until you have an ultra-smooth puree, 5 to 6 minutes. Measure the puree (you should have about 2 cups).

In a heavy-bottomed medium saucepan, mix the puree with an **equal amount of sugar, 1 tablespoon fresh lemon juice**, and **2 drops lavender oil**. Cook over medium-low heat for 45 minutes, stirring every 5 minutes or so in the beginning and then almost continuously once you're halfway through. When the paste is thick enough to hold its shape (think of the "stiff peaks" of beaten egg whites), evenly spread it in a greased 8 x 8-inch baking pan. Let set for 4 hours, then cut into sixteen 2-inch squares.

Makes 16 pieces. Store in the refrigerator tightly wrapped in wax paper and plastic wrap for up to 3 months. Yummy with many cheeses, including **Manchego** (see page 116), **Dorset** (see page 87), **Le Charmoix** (see page 78), and **Mahon** (see page 116). As an intact slab, makes an excellent host gift.

BLEATING HEART CHEESE FAT BOTTOM GIRL
Notes of caramel, beeswax, and cured sausage, with a hard, granular paste and washed/ natural rind

Fat Bottom Girl derives its name from the classic Queen song, an homage to the cheese's rotund shape, which is "fatter" on the bottom. Distinct smoked meat and tropical fruit notes combine forces to pull off a *tacos al pastor* vibe. A slightly dry paste is just shy of beeswaxy, with a nice toothsome nibble.

BLACK & WHITE SESAME CRISPS
You'll need black and white sesame seeds, light corn syrup

Nutty, sweet, crunchy, and visually appealing, these crisps are a stylish pairing for Fat Bottom Girl. Sometimes a simple, good-looking pairing is enough—the nutty crisps find kindred notes in the cheese, and are a platform for the fruity/meaty tones of the cheese.

Preheat the oven to 350°F. Line a baking sheet with parchment paper.

Mix **¼ cup black sesame seeds** and **¼ cup white sesame seeds** with **¼ cup light corn syrup** and **¼ teaspoon kosher salt**. Spread over the prepared baking sheet with an oiled offset spatula into a ¼-inch-thick sheet.

Bake for 10 to 12 minutes, until the sesame seeds start to color. Cool for 5 minutes in the pan, then carefully transfer to a wire rack to finish cooling. Break into pieces and store in between layers of parchment paper in an airtight container.

Makes 8 large crisps. Store in a cool, dry place for up to 1 week. Also keen on **Ardrahan** (see page 158).

EWEPHORIA AGED
Pasteurized Sheep's Milk
East Friesland, The Netherlands

SPICED CORN NUT BRITTLE

CYPRESS GROVE CHEVRE LAMB CHOPPER
Pasteurized Sheep's Milk
The Netherlands

GRACE & I HARVEST FRUIT + NUT PRESS

CENTRAL COAST CREAMERY GOAT GOUDA
Pasteurized Goat's Milk
Paso Robles, California

DATE-GLAZED BABY EGGPLANT WITH ORANGE & FENNEL

GOUDA-ESQUE

The dulcet flavors of Gouda-style cheeses are just right for those who prefer firm, toasty "table cheeses." Dutch Goudas (see **L'Amuse Goudas**, page 111) are traditionally made with cow's milk, but the global popularity of the Gouda style has spawned a new generation of goat's- and sheep's milk versions—a boon for those unable to tolerate cow's milk or who prefer less gamy goat and sheep's milk cheeses. Playful condiments with plenty of texture and seasoning elevate this flight to more than just safe snacking.

CENTRAL COAST CREAMERY GOAT GOUDA
Notes of yogurt and candied lemon peel with a hard, flaky paste and waxed rind

Central Coast Creamery Goat Gouda is a tangy, straightforward cheese made from goat's milk and cream. Aged for five months, it hits all the reliable notes of an accessible goat's milk Gouda: sweet and crunchy, with just a touch of goat funk and a long, caramelized finish.

DATE-GLAZED BABY EGGPLANT WITH ORANGE & FENNEL
You'll need olive oil, date syrup, orange, balsamic vinegar, baby eggplant, fennel seeds

Baby eggplants are the perfect scale for composed cheese plates, and they're as creamy, silky, and earthy as their full-size cousins. They add a dose of complexity to goat Gouda without detracting from its simple charm, and they sure are cute on the plate. The date syrup glaze mirrors the nutty sweetness of the cheese, while the orange and fennel enliven it with zesty floral flavors. Used like honey, **Date Lady Date Syrup** is a wonderful, molasses-y accompaniment in its own right.

Preheat the broiler. Line a baking sheet with a silicone baking mat.

In a medium bowl, whisk together **1 tablespoon olive oil**, **1 tablespoon date syrup** (I use **Date Lady Date Syrup**), **1 tablespoon orange zest**, **1 teaspoon fresh orange juice**, and **½ teaspoon balsamic vinegar**. Season with salt and freshly ground black pepper.

Halve **4 baby eggplant** lengthwise and add them to the bowl. Marinate for 5 minutes, then place cut side down on the prepared baking sheet; reserve the marinade. Broil until the eggplants darken, about 7 minutes. Turn, brush with the remaining marinade, and sprinkle with **1 teaspoon fennel seeds**. Broil until browned and soft, 7 minutes or so more. Serve warm or at room temperature, 1 eggplant per cheese plate. Can be made 1 day ahead and stored in the refrigerator.

Makes 8. Also a great match with **Quadrello di Bufala** (see page 70) and **Pecorino Brigantaccio** (see page 163). Lovely in arugula salad, with toasted pine nuts, chopped dates, and more of the date marinade.

CYPRESS GROVE CHEVRE LAMB CHOPPER
Notes of caramel and brown butter, with a firm, smooth paste and waxed rind

Lamb Chopper is the triumphant offspring of a partnership between American and Dutch cheese makers. This young, supple, sweet, nutty, Gouda-style cheese has international cred and universal appeal, and is a gentle introduction to sheep's milk cheese. It'd be hard to find someone who wouldn't enjoy it.

Grace & I Harvest Fruit + Nut Press is a mix of sliced persimmons and quince with pecans, walnuts, and almonds. The mellow, honeyed sweetness of the persimmon, the tart floral of the quince, and the round richness of the three nuts are a fine match for Lamb Chopper, highlighting similar notes in the cheese while adding a crunchy, sticky, and frankly stunning element to the composition. Fantastic with so many cheeses, including **Bûcheron** (see page 66), **Manchego** (see page 116), and **Monte Enebro** (see page 75).

EWEPHORIA AGED

Notes of butterscotch pudding and cashews, with a hard, crystalline paste and waxed rind

Ewephoria is a crystalline powerhouse with an almost candy-like sweetness. That's right: *cheese candy*. Aged nine months. Addictive.

SPICED CORN NUT BRITTLE

You'll need sugar, light corn syrup, unsalted butter, baking soda, spiced corn nuts

Brittle is a fantastic medium to deliver spiciness that on its own could overpower the cheese; its caramel sweetness appeases the heat. The brittle's crunch is an excellent match for Ewephoria, which is pretty crunchy as far as cheese goes.

Line a baking sheet with ½-inch sides with lightly oiled parchment paper.

In a large, heavy-bottomed saucepan, combine **1 cup sugar, ½ cup light corn syrup**, and **½ cup water** and cook over medium heat until the caramel turns light brown and reaches 320°F on a candy thermometer. Remove from the heat and stir in **1½ tablespoons butter, ½ teaspoon baking soda**, and **½ teaspoon kosher salt** with a heatproof spatula (proceed with caution, as the mixture will bubble and expand).

Pour the mixture onto the prepared baking sheet and quickly and evenly spread it with an oiled heatproof spatula. Sprinkle **1 cup spiced corn nuts** onto the hot brittle, gently pressing them into the brittle with the spatula.

Cool on the baking sheet on a wire rack. Break into shards before serving.

Makes 1 pound. Store in between layers of parchment paper in an airtight container in a cool, dry place for up to 1 month. Sidles up nicely to **Mimolette** (see page 150).

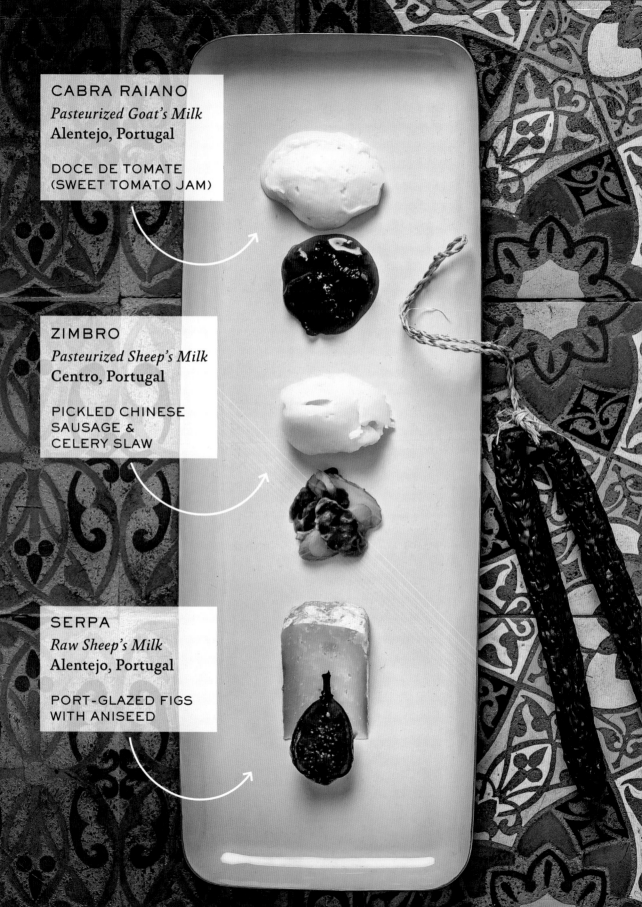

CABRA RAIANO
Pasteurized Goat's Milk
Alentejo, Portugal

DOCE DE TOMATE
(SWEET TOMATO JAM)

ZIMBRO
Pasteurized Sheep's Milk
Centro, Portugal

PICKLED CHINESE
SAUSAGE &
CELERY SLAW

SERPA
Raw Sheep's Milk
Alentejo, Portugal

PORT-GLAZED FIGS
WITH ANISEED

PORTUGUEEZY

Across regions and milk types, Portuguese cheeses express a unique terroir, a combination of the rocky interior and the sunny, salt-sprayed coast that captures the soul of the land. Torta-style cheeses—unique to Portugal and its neighbor, Spain—are sexy and sour, with a silky, pudding-y texture. Rustic, hard cheeses wear their barnyard funk proudly. Sometimes tougher to find than their Spanish cousins, Portuguese cheeses are worth snatching up when you see them.

CABRA RAIANO
Notes of roasted root vegetables, lemon marmalade, and sour milk with a pudding-like paste and natural/waxed rind

A *torta*-style goat cheese, Cabra Raiano's custardy paste is distinctive from the moist/chalky goat cheeses of France and the United States. The acidic twang of goat's milk is delivered in a velvety, sour, whipped cloud, a fantastic canvas for subtle vegetal/herbal flavors. Avoid Cabra Raiano's rind—it's not meant for eating.

DOCE DE TOMATE (SWEET TOMATO JAM)
You'll need lemon, plum tomato, sugar, bay leaf, cinnamon stick

Doce de tomate is a traditional Portuguese jam that's a bright companion to the cheeses that inevitably appear before and after the main meal. Kissed with the woodsy, herbal flavors of cinnamon and bay leaf, it's a candy-apple-red showstopper that's easy to make and that plays well with Cabra Raiano's herbal notes.

Peel **½ lemon** in large strips with a vegetable peeler.

Bring a large pot of salted water to a boil. Add **2 pounds plum tomatoes** and cook until the skins peel away, about 5 minutes. Drain and rinse under cold water until cool enough to handle. Peel, trim, and dice, removing the seeds if you'd like, although it's not necessary. Transfer the tomatoes to a heavy-bottomed medium saucepan and add **2½ cups sugar**, the lemon peel, **1 bay leaf**, **1 cinnamon stick**, and **½ teaspoon kosher salt**. Bring to a boil over medium heat, then reduce the heat to low and cook until the jam sets, about 2 hours. Cool the jam for 5 minutes, then pour into two glass ½-pint jars. Cool to room temperature, then cover tightly and refrigerate until ready to serve.

Makes 1 pint. Store in the refrigerator for up to 3 weeks. Also a great match with **Monte Enebro** (see page 75) and **Gouda "Pril"** (see page 111).

ZIMBRO
Notes of yeast, sour milk, and thyme, with a pudding-like paste and natural/waxed rind

Zimbro is a *torta*-style cheese like Cabra Raiano, but with a decidedly sheepy/funky inflection. It has the hallmarks of its style—a pudding-y texture and sour milk flavors—but wonderful lanolin and wet wool notes indicative of sheep's milk. As with Cabra Raiano, avoid the rind on this one.

PICKLED CHINESE SAUSAGE & CELERY SLAW
You'll need rice vinegar, mirin, celery seed, sesame oil, Chinese dried sausage, celery, parsley

"Chinese sausage" is a generic term for any sweet, fatty dried sausage flavored with cinnamon, star anise, and fennel.

In a medium bowl, whisk together **2 tablespoons rice vinegar, 1 tablespoon mirin,** and **½ teaspoon celery seed**. Whisk in **¼ cup sesame oil**. Add **1 sliced Chinese dried sausage** and toss to coat.

Thinly slice **2 celery stalks**, reserving the leaves. Toss the sliced celery with the dressing and marinate for 1 hour. Season with salt and freshly cracked black pepper, and garnish with **celery and parsley leaves**. Serve immediately.

Makes 1 cup. Also a great match with **Barilotto** (see page 70) and **Fat Bottom Girl** (see page 125).

SERPA
Notes of burnt sugar, sheep sweat, and damp earth, with a hard, flaky paste and natural rind

Serpa can see up to two years of maturation; older wheels are spicy and aggressively animally, while younger wheels proffer softer herbal/grassy notes amid sheepy tones.

PORT-GLAZED FIGS WITH ANISEED
You'll need Mission figs, sugar, unsalted butter, lemon, aniseeds, ruby port

Serpa is done right by a sweet pairing. With its concentrated dark fruit flavors, port ramps up the sweetness of the figs, while the anise adds a round herbal note, coaxing similar herbal tones from the cheese.

Halve **6 figs** and sprinkle the cut sides with **1 teaspoon sugar**. In a small sauté pan, melt **1 tablespoon butter**. Add the figs, raise the heat to medium-high, and cook cut side down, without stirring, until browned, 3 to 4 minutes. Reduce the heat to medium and sprinkle the figs with the **zest of ¼ lemon** and **½ teaspoon aniseeds**. Pour **¼ cup ruby port** over the figs and cook until the port has reduced into a thick glaze, 2 to 3 minutes. Remove from the heat and serve immediately.

Makes 12. A sinful match with **Gorgonzola Cremificato** (see page 00).

DRINK ME
Niepoort 10 Years Old Tawny Port
Blend of traditional port grapes, Duoro, Portugal
Medium body, with notes of orange peel and dried apricot

Fonseca Late Bottled Vintage Ruby Port
Blend of traditional Port grapes, Duoro, Portugal
Full body, with notes of dark chocolate, blackberry compote, and vanilla

MONTGOMERY'S CHEDDAR

Raw Cow's Milk
Somerset, England

MORE MODERN
MINCEMEAT

LOVE LETTER TO CLOTHBOUND CHEDDAR

Three superlative examples of iconic savory, sweet, and meaty clothbound cheddar are prime for punked-out pairings in this flight for cheddar fanatics and the clothbound curious.

CABOT CREAMERY CLOTHBOUND CHEDDAR
Raw Cow's Milk
Vermont

VERMONT SMOKE & CURE SUMMER SAUSAGE, TIN WHOLEGRAIN MUSTARD

BLEU MONT DAIRY BANDAGED CHEDDAR
Pasteurized Cow's Milk
Blue Mounds, Wisconsin

CHEDDAR CHEESE STRAW BRICKLE

MONTGOMERY'S CHEDDAR
Notes of sizzling beef fat, caramelized onions, and butterscotch, with a firm, medium dry paste

Montgomery's Cheddar is one of the few British Cheddars still made using strictly traditional methods. Matured for at least one year (though some can go as long as eighteen months), younger wheels are rich and savory with caramelized sweetness, while more age releases a peppery bite and drier texture.

MORE MODERN MINCEMEAT
You'll need red onion, sugar, apple, dried fruits, crystallized ginger, orange, brown sugar, dark rum, Grand Marnier, unsalted butter, apple cider, candied mixed peel, spices

The deep, caramelized sugar and dried fruit flavors of mincemeat are the overlap in this pairing, while the juicy, boozy fruit is a complex counterpoint to the crystalline crunch and rendered fat notes of Monty's. This pairing may leave you wondering, "Is this sweet or savory?" The answer is: *yes.* Mincemeat needs at least three days in the refrigerator for the flavors to meld, so plan accordingly.

First, make quick-pickled onions:
In a small saucepan, combine **¼ cup thinly sliced red onion**, **½ cup water**, **¼ cup sugar**, and **½ teaspoon kosher salt** and bring to a simmer over medium heat. Simmer for 5 minutes. Cool to room temperature, drain, and mince.

In a heavy-bottomed medium saucepan, combine **1 grated tart apple** (such as Granny Smith, Cortland, or Braeburn), **¼ cup each dark raisins**, **golden raisins**, **dried apricots**, **cranberries**, **currants**, and **chopped dried figs**; **2 tablespoons chopped crystallized ginger**; the **zest and juice of 1 orange**; **⅓ cup packed dark brown sugar**; **2 tablespoons each dark rum**, **Grand Marnier**, and **butter**; **½ cup apple cider**; **⅓ cup candied peel**; **¼ teaspoon each cinnamon**, **nutmeg**, and **kosher salt**; and **⅛ teaspoon each ground ginger**, **cumin**, **cardamom**, and **cloves**. Cook over medium-high heat until bubbling, then reduce heat to low and cook until almost all the liquid has evaporated, about 30 minutes. Cool completely, then add the minced onions and **1 tablespoon rum**.

Refrigerate for 3 days prior serving, so the flavors have time to meld.

Makes 2 cups. Store in a nonreactive container in the refrigerator for up to 3 months. If the mincemeat starts to look a little dry during storage, top it off with more rum. Sidles up nicely to **Goat Gouda** (see page 128), **Barely Buzzed** (see page 154), **Winnimere** (see page 174), and **Irish Porter** (see page 155).

CABOT CREAMERY CLOTHBOUND CHEDDAR

Notes of chicken broth and honey mustard, with a firm, crumbly paste

Tangy/nutty/meaty with a touch of sweetness, Cabot Clothbound Cheddar is made from milk sourced exclusively from one farm, ensuring a consistency in its quality. Expertly matured for ten to fifteen months.

The sweet, salty, and umami richness of Cabot Clothbound Cheddar welcomes the tang of **Vermont Smoke & Cure Summer Sausage**, an uncured, slow-fermented beef-and-pork sausage. The two are lashed by the acidity of **Tin Wholegrain Mustard**, which also adds the pleasant pop of mustard seeds.

BLEU MONT DAIRY BANDAGED CHEDDAR

Notes of canned pineapple, bacon, and charcoal, with a hard, crumbly paste

Sweet tropical fruit notes like pineapple and mango punctuate the grilled meat flavors in this clothbound gem. The most aged cheese in this flight—with sixteen to twenty months of maturity—Bleu Mont Dairy Bandaged Cheddar boasts seemingly addictive tyrosine crystals, those crunchy bits found in hard aged cheeses like cheddar, **Gouda "Signature"** (see page 111), and **Grana Padano** (see page 150).

CHEDDAR CHEESE STRAW BRICKLE

You'll need cheese straws, sugar, unsalted butter, vanilla extract, chocolate chips

Crystallization in Bleu Mont Dairy Bandaged Cheddar is returned in kind by crunchy, salty, sweet brickle. The brown butter and chocolate flavors reach deep into the almost smoky character of the cheese.

Preheat the oven to 350°F. Line an 8-inch square cake pan with aluminum foil, leaving extra foil overhanging the edges. Place **12 (8-inch) cheese straws** in a single layer in the prepared pan, breaking a cheese straw or two if necessary so that the bottom of the pan is completely covered.

In a small saucepan, bring **½ cup sugar** and **½ cup butter** to a gentle boil over medium heat. Cook until the mixture turns light brown and has a nutty aroma, 4 to 5 minutes. Remove from the heat and add **½ teaspoon vanilla extract**.

Pour the mixture over the cheese straws and bake for 8 minutes. Remove the pan from the oven, sprinkle **1 cup semisweet chocolate chips** over the hot brickle, return the pan to the oven, and bake for 2 minutes more, or until the chocolate has completely melted. Evenly spread the chocolate with a heatproof spatula or pastry brush. Cool completely in the pan on a wire rack.

Lift the brickle from the pan by the edges of the foil. With the foil still in place, wrap the brickle tightly in plastic wrap and freeze overnight. The following day, carefully peel away the foil, wrap the brickle in plastic wrap, and freeze until ready to serve. Break the brickle into serving-size pieces and serve frozen.

Makes 20 reasonable portions or 10 unreasonable portions. Store in the freezer for up to 1 month. Also yummy with **Barely Buzzed** (see page 154).

DRINK ME

Sierra Nevada Bigfoot

Barleywine-Style Ale, Chico, California

Full body, with notes of burnt caramel, dried dark fruits, and pine sap

Barley wine is actually a beer, but as an experience it's somewhere between the two. A tangy, malty pour with savory, dark-fruit notes, it's a good match for robust clothbound cheddars, which especially adore tangy, toasty, caramel tones. The mincemeat pairing is a big winner here. Proceed with caution—Bigfoot is potent at 9.6% ABV.

SARGEANT PEPPERS

A flight liberally laced with peppers. The first two cheeses are more fruity than fiery, with peppercorn-studded pastes. But the third is a three-alarm humdinger, aimed at hotheads and spice junkies. Ingratiating accompaniments either enhance or temper these peppery pals, with ingratiating, balancing pairings.

COACH
FARM GREEN
PEPPERCORN
CONE
Pasteurized Goat's Milk
Pine Plains, NY

GREEN
PEPPERCORN
MERINGUE

BELLWETHER
FARM PEPATO
Raw Sheep's Milk
Petaluma, California

LA QUERCIA 'NDUJA

MARCELLI
FORMAGGI RICOTTA
PEPERONCINO
Raw Sheep's Milk
Abruzzo, Italy

BASIL & PRESERVED
LEMON PESTO

COACH FARM GREEN PEPPERCORN CONE
Notes of bergamot and black pepper, with a fluffy paste and white bloomy rind

Coach Farm Green Peppercorn Cone is the mildest of the three cheeses in this flight. In fact, green peppercorns aren't very spicy at all, adding subtle fruity, citrus notes to this goat cheese.

GREEN PEPPERCORN MERINGUE
You'll need dried green peppercorns, egg white, sugar

Providing you don't attempt these meringues on a humid day, they're an easy, impressive accompaniment for a tangy goat cheese: airy, sweet, crisp shards of fruity and floral peppered loveliness. Green peppercorn appears in both the cheese and the pairing, yet it's the contrast between fluffy cheese and crispy meringue that makes the pairing special.

Preheat the oven to 175°F. On a cutting board, crush **1 tablespoon dried green peppercorns** with a mortar and pestle or with the underside of a heavy pan.

In a clean, dry bowl, beat **1 egg white** and a **pinch of kosher salt** with an electric mixer at medium-high speed until soft peaks form. Increase the speed to high and gradually add **2 tablespoons sugar**, beating until the mixture is glossy and holds stiff peaks. Fold in **2 additional tablespoons sugar** with a spatula to completely combine. Be careful not to deflate by overmixing.

Dab meringue batter on the corners of a baking sheet and line with parchment paper, pressing the paper against the meringue "glue." Spread the meringue over the parchment with an offset spatula to ¼ inch thick. Sprinkle the crushed peppercorns onto the meringue and bake until crisp and dry, 1½ to 2½ hours. Baking time will depend on the amount of humidity in the air. It's best to bake meringue on dry days.

Cool on the baking sheet on a wire rack for 10 minutes, then gently peel the meringue from the parchment paper and cool completely on the rack. Store in an airtight container in a cool, dry place until ready to serve. Break into shards before serving.

Makes enough for 4 cheese plates plus goody bags. Store in a cool, dry place for up to 1 week. Tasty paired with **La Tur** (see page 106), **Valençay** (see page 65), **Bûcheron** (see page 66), and **Humboldt Fog** (see page 75). Great with fruit sorbets, like raspberry or mango.

BELLWETHER FARM PEPATO
Notes of butterscotch and black pepper, with a hard, crumbly paste and natural rind

The whole black peppercorns in Bellwether Farm Pepato are studded throughout its paste with layers of nutty/fruity flavors. Pepato's sheepy funk is subtle: It's no James Brown, but the peppercorns do their part to spice things up.

La Quercia 'Nduja is a spicy Italian pork sausage made without a casing and completely spreadable. Cured prosciutto, speck, and red chile peppers sharpen the bite of this pairing, while the moist texture of the 'nduja contrasts Pepato's hard, crumbly paste.

MARCELLI FORMAGGI RICOTTA PEPERONCINO
Notes of sheep sweat and red hot chile peppers, with a dense, fudge-like paste and a chile-crusted exterior

Marcelli Formaggi Ricotta Peperoncino is a one-of-a-kind-cheese, made on a small family farm in one of Italy's most famous sheep's milk cheese regions. It's gently cold-smoked with juniper wood and crusted with Italian peperoncino—a cheese with a bracing hit of fiery heat and plenty of funky, sheepy flavors, smoothed out by the fruit tones of the smoke. It's worth seeking out online for its handcrafted vibe and assertive singularity.

BASIL & PRESERVED LEMON PESTO
You'll need pecans, basil, garlic, lemon, preserved lemon, anchovy paste, red pepper flakes, extra-virgin olive oil

Easy to make, endlessly adaptable, and full of cheese-friendly, concentrated fresh herb flavors, pesto is an indispensible sauce in pairing. Preserved lemon adds a floral quality to this version, in which the bright citrus and herbal flavors tame the sheepy heat of Ricotta Peperoncino. Toasted pecans add an undertone of nutty richness.

In a food processor, combine **1/3 cup toasted pecans, 4 cups tightly packed basil leaves, 1 garlic clove**, the **zest and juice of 2 lemons, 1 teaspoon minced preserved lemon, 1/2 teaspoon anchovy paste**, and **1/2 teaspoon red pepper flakes** and pulse until coarsely chopped. Add **1/4 cup extra-virgin olive oil** and pulse until smooth. Season with salt and freshly cracked black pepper.

Makes 1 cup. Store in the refrigerator, its surface covered with a thin layer of olive oil and tightly sealed, for up to 2 weeks. Also keen on **Brebirousse d'Argental** (see page 50), **Ledyard** (see page 87), and **Plain Young Gouda** (see page 110). Excellent tossed with potatoes for roasting.

SMOKY BANDITS

Smoked cheeses are either loved or loathed—an unfortunate legacy of the "liquid smoke" used in cheeses of lesser quality. But great cheese, expertly smoked with real wood, lingers on the palate like a shadow, a flavor that recalls our primal relationship with fire. Sweet, sour, and spicy accompaniments are a foil for these hunks of burning love.

SALVATORE BKLYN SMOKED WHOLE MILK RICOTTA
Pasteurized Cow's Milk
Brooklyn, New York

PAN-ROASTED PLUMS WITH SCOTCH & LIME

IDIAZABAL
Raw Sheep's Milk
Basque and Navarre Regions, Spain

RICK'S PICKS "SMOKRA"

ROGUE CREAMERY SMOKEY BLUE
Raw Cow's Milk
Central Point, Oregon

OLYMPIA PROVISIONS SALCHICHÓN DE CHOCOLAT

SALVATORE BKLYN SMOKED WHOLE MILK RICOTTA
Notes of charred marshmallow, fresh cream, and cherrywood smoke, with a creamy, rich curd

Salvatore Bklyn Smoked Whole Milk Ricotta is made with heavy cream and lemon juice, and is so rich that the sweet cherrywood smoke actually tempers its butterfat intensity. Clean, milky flavors are front and center here, while smokiness lingers in the background like the scent of campfire.

PAN-ROASTED PLUMS WITH SCOTCH & LIME
You'll need Scotch, honey, lime, vanilla bean, unsalted butter, cinnamon stick, plums

Small, tart plums like damsons or just-shy-of-ripe French prunes (aka sugar plums) are recommended here, as they maintain their shape and aren't too sweet. A peaty single-malt Scotch adds a complex smoky counterpoint to the plums, lending an alternate tone of smokiness to the ricotta.

In a small bowl, whisk together **1 tablespoon smoky single-malt Scotch** (I use **Laphroaig**), **1 tablespoon honey**, the **zest of ½ lime**, **seeds from 1 vanilla bean**, and a **pinch of kosher salt**.

In a medium sauté pan, melt **1 tablespoon butter** over medium heat until foaming. Add **1 cinnamon stick** and **12 halved pitted small ripe plums**, cut-side down. Cook, undisturbed, for 3 to 4 minutes. Raise the heat to high and pour the Scotch-honey mixture into the pan, agitating the pan to evenly coat the plums. Cook until the plums are well coated and the sauce is syrupy, 2 to 3 minutes. The ideal serving here is 4 plum halves, drizzled with pan juices. *Makes 24, including leftovers.*

Makes enough for 4 cheese plates of 2 plums each, plus leftovers. Wouldn't kick **La Tur** (see page 106) or **Smokey Blue** (see page 147) out of bed. Delicious with crème fraîche and toasted almonds or crumbled amaretti cookies.

IDIAZABAL
Notes of smoked ham, wood fire, and wool, with a hard, granular paste and natural rind

Idiazabal has a particular pungent, fatty essence that only sheep's milk could make. Traditionally, it's matured in the wood rafters of shepherds' homes, where it absorbs the smoke from perpetually lit fireplaces. Modern Idiazabal maintains that subtle smokiness, though maturation methods have modernized.

Okra's such a unique-looking vegetable—like all mini veg it's darling on cheese plates. Serving it can be a tricky, as some folks definitely have an aversion to it, but when pickled it's capable of converting naysayers. **Rick's Picks Smokra** is a smoked, spicy, tangy, and earthy accompaniment that reinforces the subtle smoky notes latent in Idiazabal. Bursting with juicy heat.

ROGUE CREAMERY SMOKEY BLUE
Notes of bacon, seaweed, and green banana, with a moist, smooth paste

Rogue Smokey Blue has a lightness that can only be attributed to the quality of its milk and moist, curdy texture. The hazelnut shells used to cold-smoke it add a fresh smoke flavor that's more chestnuts on an open fire than stop, drop, and roll.

Say it with me now: Chocolate. Sausage. That's right: **Olympia Provisions Salchichón de Chocolat** is a rich chocolate ganache sausage studded with pistachios and candied grapefruit seasoned with smoked paprika and sherry. It's a sweet, smoky, umami match for Smokey Blue, as well as a fun, surprising element on a cheese plate.

DRINK ME
Aecht Schlenkerla Rauchbier
Rauchbier, Bamberg, Germany
Medium body, with notes of smoked hay, Demerara sugar, and Canadian bacon

A singular beer made in an old, traditional smoked style by a historic German brewery. Spicy malt notes are an interesting contribution to the smoked theme of the flight. Especially yummy with the **Smokey Blue** and **Salchichón de Chocolat**.

HARD DAY'S NIGHT

When only a stiff drink will do, hard cheeses have the chutzpah to tangle with booze. The concentrated flavors in these aged cheeses work in concert with cocktails: The drinks stimulate the appetite, while the savory, salty cheese makes you want another sip. Enjoy this flight with any one of the cocktails, or if you're feeling particularly flush, all three.

GIN NEGRONI

GRANA PADANO
RISERVA
Raw Cow's Milk
Po River Valley, Italy

COGNAC SIDECAR

MIMOLETTE
Raw Cow's Milk
Lille, France

AMARO MONTENEGRO

BIANCO SARDO
Raw Sheep's Milk
Sardinia, Italy

GRANA PADANO RISERVA

Notes of roasted game bird, tangerine zest, and hazelnut, with a creamy, hard, dry paste

Grana Padano was first made by monks more than nine hundred years ago using a recipe similar to Parmigiano Reggiano. "Grana" refers to the grainy texture of this ancient cheese, and "Riserva" means it's matured over twenty months. Grana Padano has abundant crystallization with deep, hearty, toasted hay flavors.

GIN NEGRONI

You'll need gin, Campari, sweet vermouth, orange

An *aperitivo* (from the Latin *aperire*, "to open") prepares the stomach for eating—and it's safe to say the Italians know a thing or two about eating. A perfect balance of bitter and sweet, the Negroni's viscosity is handy when grappling with Grana Padano's hard, dry, granular paste.

Combine **1 ounce gin**, **1 ounce Campari**, and **1 ounce sweet vermouth** in a rocks glass with ice. Stir a couple of times and garnish with an **orange peel**.

For a booze-free pairing, try **Grana Padano Riserva** *with* **Sorrel Pesto** *(see page 23),* **Port-Glazed Figs with Aniseed** *(see page 133), or* **Ajvar** *(see page 111).*

MIMOLETTE

Notes of mustard, green bell pepper, and beeswax, with a waxy, dense paste and natural rind

Both inside and out, Mimolette's a looker: The hard, waxy paste is colored a deep orange by annatto, and the dusty, cratered rind is the handiwork of "cheese mites"—minuscule critters who munch the rind of this orb-shaped cheese, influencing the planetoid look of the rind and adding earthy notes to the cheese.

COGNAC SIDECAR
You'll need superfine sugar, lemon, cognac, Cointreau

The Sidecar was invented in the 1920s, taking its name from the motorcycle attachment symbolic of the adventuresome, freewheeling era. Fruity, nutty, caramelized cognac is softened by orange liqueur, lemon juice, and a touch of sugar in this classic cocktail, providing a bright foil for Mimolette's concentrated nutty/earthy notes.

Spread **2 tablespoons superfine sugar** over a small plate. Rub the rim of a coupe or martini glass with a **wedge of lemon** and roll the rim in the sugar to coat. Combine **1½ ounces cognac**, **1 ounce Cointreau**, **1 tablespoon fresh lemon juice**, and **ice** in a cocktail shaker. Shake vigorously, strain into the prepared glass, and serve immediately.

For a booze-free pairing, try **Mimolette** *with* **Spiced Corn Nut Brittle** *(see page 129),* **Sticky Tamarind-Glazed Brazil Nuts** *(see page 70), or* **Brooklyn Brine Damn Spicy Pickles** *(see page 159).*

BIANCO SARDO
Notes of walnuts and eucalyptus, with a granular, slightly oily paste and natural rind

On the island of Sardinia, sheep and goats outnumber humans. This is the land of Bianco Sardo, a sweet, barnyardy sheep's milk cheese with a crumbly, slightly oily paste. Amaro Montenegro draws out its herbal/citrus notes and mimics the caramel and burnt sugar undertones.

Amaro Montenegro from Bologna is an excellent introduction to the complex world of Italian amaro, a brandy-based *digestivo* infused with herbs and spices. Unlike some more bitter iterations, Montenegro is light and balanced, with a round, flavorful sweetness. It's made with more than forty herbs: rose, lavender, orange peel, and allspice flavors are layered in this complex sipper.

For a booze-free pairing, try **Bianco Sardo** *with* **Better Wet Walnuts** *(see page 162),* **Pickled Chinese Sausage & Celery Slaw** *(see page 132), or* **Date Lady Date Syrup** *(see page 128).*

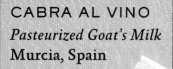

CABRA AL VINO
Pasteurized Goat's Milk
Murcia, Spain

CREMINELLI SALAME
AL BAROLO

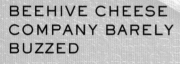

BEEHIVE CHEESE
COMPANY BARELY
BUZZED
Pasteurized Cow's Milk
Uintah, Utah

DARK CHOCOLATE-
ESPRESSO GANACHE

CAHILL'S IRISH
PORTER
Pasteurized Cow's Milk
County Limerick, Ireland

GLAZED MEDJOOL
DATES

VICE

If this is wrong, let's never be right. Cheeses infused with beer, wine, and coffee demonstrate that a little bit of vice is the spice of life. Share with risk-takers, stimulant lovers, and cheese addicts.

CABRA AL VINO
Notes of hazelnuts and prune, with a firm, dense paste and purple rind

Literally "goat in wine" (also referred to as "drunken goat"), Cabra al Vino is an approachable, über-snacky cheese—a perfect beginning to a debaucherous cheese plate. Cabra al Vino takes a three-day bath in red wine, emerging with a glorious purple-hued rind that looks fab on a cheese plate, while its paste remains the characteristic bright white of goat cheese, with nutty/sweet flavors.

Red wine–infused sausage is a logical pairing for a red wine–soaked cheese. *Creminelli Salame al Barolo* delivers meaty/fruity flavors in a toothsome rich, cured pork sausage. Also tasty paired with **Pecorinos** (see pages 162 to 163).

BEEHIVE CHEESE COMPANY BARELY BUZZED
Notes of butterscotch and peanuts, with a firm paste and espresso-and-lavender-crusted rind

Therein lies the rub: Barely Buzzed is a whimsical blend of tradition and innovation, a cheddar-style cheese crusted in ground espresso beans and lavender. Grassy/caramel flavors veer from the status quo with the floral, chocolate, and coffee notes of the aromatic dry rub.

DARK CHOCOLATE–ESPRESSO GANACHE
You'll need dark chocolate, heavy cream, espresso, vanilla extract

I've always paired Barely Buzzed with dark chocolate—it's a spectacular pairing—and ganache is a great vehicle for delivering concentrated dark chocolate flavors while playing on the smooth, rich textures of butterfat. Look for a dark chocolate with floral notes, to pick up the lavender in the cheese.

Chop **7 ounces dark chocolate** (over 60% cacao) very fine (this will help it melt quickly) and place in a heatproof medium bowl.

In a small saucepan, cook **¼ cup heavy cream** and **2 tablespoons brewed espresso** over low heat until the edges of the mixture bubble. Pour the cream over the chopped chocolate and let sit for a minute or two. Whisk thoroughly to incorporate the chocolate into the cream. Whisk in **½ teaspoon vanilla extract** and **¼ teaspoon kosher salt**.

The ganache will be runny; refrigerate for 30 minutes or so to firm the ganache to the consistency of creamy peanut butter. Stir every 10 minutes so it chills evenly. If the ganache gets too cold and firm, let it sit at room temperature until it's workable again.

Makes 1 cup. Tasty with **Valdeon** (see page 33) and **Grevenbroecker** (see page 79).

CAHILL'S IRISH PORTER
Notes of malt and molasses with a firm, smooth paste and waxed rind

Cahill's Irish Porter is a looker: a marbled amalgam of cheese curd and porter beer with a dense paste of malted-milk goodness. Tangy tones linger harmoniously with the molasses notes of the beer.

GLAZED MEDJOOL DATES
You'll need Medjool dates, brown sugar, molasses, tomato paste, cocoa powder, malt vinegar, smooth mustard

The deep molasses flavors of Cahill's Irish Porter come alive with these sticky and sweet glazed dates. Tomato paste and cocoa powder add a savory undercurrent to this humble pairing.

Position a rack in the center of the oven and preheat the broiler. Line a baking sheet with parchment paper. Place **6 halved pitted Medjool dates** cut-side up on the baking sheet.

In a small bowl, whisk together **1 teaspoon dark brown sugar, 1 teaspoon molasses, 1 teaspoon tomato paste, ½ teaspoon cocoa powder, ½ teaspoon malt vinegar, ½ teaspoon smooth mustard** (I used **Tin Smooth Mustard**), and freshly cracked black pepper.

Brush the dates with the glaze and broil until it bubbles and caramelizes, 3 minutes. Flip, brush with more glaze, and broil until tender, sticky, and browned, 3 to 5 minutes. Serve warm or at room temperature.

Makes enough for 4 cheese plates of 3 date halves each. Store in a sealed container, in a cool, dry place for up to 3 days. Wouldn't kick a **Clothbound Cheddar** (see pages 137 to 138) out of bed.

DRINK ME
Founders Brewing Company Founders' Porter
American porter, Grand Rapids, Michigan
Full body, with notes of cold brew coffee, chocolate, and malt

This tasty brew plays on many of the flavors threaded throughout this flight. It's an especially fine match for the **Barely Buzzed** and **Dark Chocolate–Espresso Ganache** and the **Cahill's Irish Porter** and **Glazed Medjool Dates**.

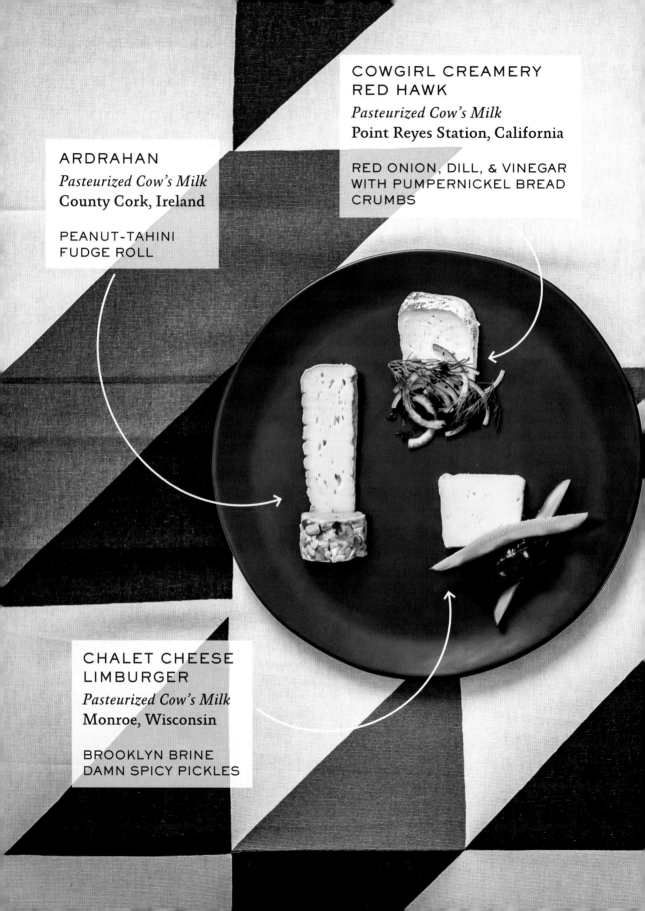

ARDRAHAN
Pasteurized Cow's Milk
County Cork, Ireland

PEANUT-TAHINI
FUDGE ROLL

COWGIRL CREAMERY
RED HAWK
Pasteurized Cow's Milk
Point Reyes Station, California

RED ONION, DILL, & VINEGAR
WITH PUMPERNICKEL BREAD
CRUMBS

CHALET CHEESE
LIMBURGER
Pasteurized Cow's Milk
Monroe, Wisconsin

BROOKLYN BRINE
DAMN SPICY PICKLES

STANKONIA

Stinky cheeses are as compelling as the odor that precedes them, but those odors can be misleading. A cheese is rarely as forceful as its aroma, though it's true that washed cheeses can pack a punch. Even so, they rarely taste like dirty socks as much as they smell like them. High-acid pairings are a must to mollify this funky bunch, but intense sweetness is also a worthwhile direction; both are featured here. Serve to funk-soul lovers, with a side of breath mints to quell the aftermath.

ARDRAHAN
Notes of peanut, yeast rolls, and saline, with a silky, pliable paste and orange-hued washed rind

Ardrahan's paste is like really buttery scrambled eggs—a sensual characteristic of some washed cheeses. Notes of salted peanut and toasted seaweed give this Irish gem a cheese-as-sushi vibe.

PEANUT-TAHINI FUDGE ROLL
You'll need salted peanuts, unsalted butter, chunky peanut butter, tahini, vanilla extract, confectioners' sugar

Sometimes a cheese has such a distinctive underlying flavor that the pairing seems obvious. I rarely pair Ardrahan with anything other than peanuts. Flavor mimicry and textural contrast are the keys to success here: the fudge is as smooth and seductive as the Ardrahan, but it's really the crunchy, crushed peanuts that beguile.

Chop **⅓ cup salted peanuts** and set aside.

In a small saucepan, heat **¼ cup butter**, **½ cup chunky peanut butter**, and **¼ cup tahini paste** over low heat, whisking intermittently until the mixture is completely melted and well combined. Remove from the heat, add **1 tablespoon vanilla extract** and **1¼ cups sifted confectioners' sugar** and mix with a wooden spoon until thoroughly combined (the mixture will be quite stiff).

Divide the fudge into two balls (the fudge will be hot, so be careful and work quickly). Place one ball of fudge on a piece of parchment paper, shape into a 6-inch by 2-inch cylinder, then sprinkle evenly on all sides with half the chopped peanuts. Roll the parchment paper, twisting the ends of the paper to form a compact cylinder. Repeat with the second ball and remaining peanuts. Refrigerate the rolls for 3 hours, then slice, temper for 20 minutes or so, and serve.

Makes 2 rolls; half a roll makes enough for 4 cheese plates. Store in the refrigerator for up to 1 week. Excellent with **Saint-Nectaire** (see page 41) and **Lamb Chopper** (see page 128). There will be leftovers; send them home with guests.

COWGIRL CREAMERY RED HAWK
Notes of roasted potato skin, fresh cabbage, and crème fraîche, with a dense, triple-cream paste and red-hued washed rind

Red Hawk derives its name from it signature red-hued rind, which contributes a fine, gritty texture to the creamy, fudgy paste. Red Hawk has a rich potato frittata vibe when on the younger side, and oniony potato pancake notes when more aged.

RED ONION, DILL, & VINEGAR WITH PUMPERNICKEL BREAD CRUMBS

You'll need red onion, distilled white vinegar, pumpernickel bread, caraway seed, garlic powder, unsalted butter, fresh dill

A simple preparation inspired by a classic Bavarian appetizer that's all about creating a "third taste." Silky butterfat, sweet onions, fresh dill, and bracing vinegar converge into a crave-worthy sour, sweet, and funky bite that boasts both a light freshness and a deep richness. Red Hawk is particularly well-suited to this treatment, as the density of its triple cream paste remains intact even after a good soaking in vinegar. Pumpernickel bread crumbs add a savory, garlicky crunch.

For the cheese:
Several hours before serving, place **1 Cowgirl Creamery Red Hawk** in a glass baking dish and smother with **½ thinly sliced red onion** and **1 cup distilled white vinegar**. Refrigerate for up to six hours and baste with the vinegar every hour or so, or whenever you happen to walk past it—there's no such thing as too much basting.

For the pumpernickel bread crumbs:
In a food processor, combine **½ cup cubed stale pumpernickel bread**, **½ teaspoon caraway seed**, and **½ teaspoon garlic powder** and pulse into coarse bread crumbs.

In a small sauté pan, melt **1 tablespoon butter** over medium heat until foaming. Toast the bread crumbs in the butter until crisp. Drain on a paper towel.

Remove the cheese from the refrigerator 1 hour prior to serving and cover with heaps of **fresh dill**. Give a few cracks of black pepper. Portion and sprinkle with the pumpernickel bread crumbs.

CHALET CHEESE LIMBURGER

Notes of stinky feet and charcoal, with a dense, pliable, creamy paste and washed rind

Limburger landed in the United States in the nineteenth century via German immigrants. It became an iconic symbol of the American melting pot, only to have its funk fall out of taste during the postwar 1950s. Today, only one American producer of Limburger remains. A smooth, creamy texture delivers robust funky flavors.

Crisp **Brooklyn Brine Damn Spicy Pickles** contrast the smooth, velvety texture of Limburger while their sour, fiery heat tames the funk of the cheese without dominating it.

PECORINO ROSSO

Raw Sheep's Milk
Campania, Italy

OLLI SALUMERIA HOT
CALABRESE SALAMI

PECORINO FOGLIE DI NOCE

Raw Sheep's Milk
Emilia-Romagna, Italy

BETTER WET WALNUTS

MARCELLI FORMAGGI PECORINO BRIGANTACCIO

Raw Sheep's Milk
Abruzzo, Italy

BRAN CEREAL CRACKERS

PECORINO PRESERVATION SOCIETY

One thing is true when it comes to pecorinos: They're Italian sheep's milk cheeses (*pecora* means "sheep" in Italian). Otherwise they run the gamut from young and mild to aged and downright funky. This flight explores a fun subgenre of this massive category: mature pecorinos treated with spices, herbs, leaves, or grains that imbue the cheese with subtle flavor.

PECORINO ROSSO

Notes of sweet peppers and caramel, with a smooth, pliable paste. Rubbed with crushed Senise pepper

Pecorino Rosso has grassy/hay notes dappled with sweet, smoky of southern Italy's Senise peppers. Dried Senise are crushed and applied to Rosso's rind, which dyes it bright red. A mild pecorino with round sheepy notes more caramel and wool than straight-up barnyard, Rosso is an approachable choice for a mature pecorino.

Olli Salumeria Calabrese Salami helps the subtle sweet and smoky flavors of Rosso shine. This dry-cured pork salami made with cayenne pepper and paprika answers the call of Pecorino Rosso's smooth, sweet paste with a rich, meaty bite.

PECORINO FOGLIE DI NOCE

Notes of fresh walnut and wet wool with a moist, crumbly paste and natural rind enrobed in walnut leaves.

Pecorino Foglie di Noce is a tangy, salty, buttery pecorino that's characteristically robust but not overpowering. Prominent notes of both fresh and roasted nuts soften Foglie di Noce's funky/barnyardy flavors.

BETTER WET WALNUTS

You'll need walnuts, cinnamon stick, star anise, black peppercorns, light corn syrup, extra-dark maple syrup, vanilla bean

Since Pecorino di Fogle Noce is aged in walnut leaves, it's prime for a walnut pairing. Star anise and black pepper add licorice and spiced undertones to this classic ice cream topping. High-quality walnuts and excellent dark maple syrup are key to this simple yet sophisticated recipe, distinct from the overly sweet iterations found in supermarkets. The deep woodsy/floral flavors of walnuts draw out the same in the pecorino, while their sticky, toothsome texture plays well against the firm, slightly moist cheese.

Preheat the oven to 350°F. Line a baking sheet with parchment paper. Spread **2 cups walnut halves** over the baking sheet and toast until they just start to turn light brown, 8 to 9 minutes. Cool.

Tie **1 cinnamon stick**, **6 star anise**, and **1 teaspoon black peppercorns** into a sachet using a piece of cheesecloth and trussing string.

In a medium saucepan, combine **1 cup light corn syrup**, **1 cup extra-dark maple syrup**, and the spice sachet and bring to just below a boil over medium heat. Add the toasted walnuts, **1 split vanilla bean**, and **¼ teaspoon kosher salt** and cook until the walnuts are warmed through, 5 minutes. Cool to room temperature before serving.

Makes 2½ cups. Store in a cool, dry place for up to 2 months. Tasty paired with **Bianco Sardo** (see page 151) and **Classic Blue Log** (see page 178). Needless to say, also fantastic on ice cream.

MARCELLI FORMAGGI PECORINO BRIGANTACCIO
Notes of toasted wheat, wet clay, and mutton fat, with a moist, crumbly paste.

So ferociously funky it's practically feral, Pecorino Brigantaccio is a singular example of a pecorino, with primitive, primal flavors. Packed in bran while it ages fifteen to twenty-two months, its barnyard and sheep musk notes burst through a paste so tangy it's almost spicy. Flakes of crushed bran inevitably linger on the rind, adding an additional layer of rustic texture.

BRAN CEREAL CRACKERS
You'll need processed bran cereal, rice flour, all-purpose flour, baking powder, poppy seeds, buttermilk

An easy cracker made with the "cheat" of processed cereal. The cereal's built-in sweetness reinforces Brigantaccio's toasted bran flavors, while poppy seeds bring earthiness and a bit of texture. Thin is in when it comes to theses crackers: Roll them out to ⅛ inch thick so they bake off nice and crisp. A drizzle of **Bee Raw Buckwheat Honey** (see page 163) is a tasty add-on.

Preheat the oven to 350°F. Line a baking sheet with parchment paper.

Pulse **1 cup processed bran cereal** (I use All Bran) in a food processor. Transfer to a medium bowl and mix with **½ cup rice flour**, **½ cup all-purpose flour**, **½ teaspoon baking powder**, **2 tablespoons poppy seeds**, and **½ teaspoon kosher salt**. Slowly stir in **¾ cup buttermilk** with a wooden spoon, but finish mixing the dough by hand. It should be cohesive but not sticky—add a touch more buttermilk if you need to bring it together.

Dust a cutting board with flour and divide the dough into 3 balls. Roll into ⅛-inch-thick sheets and cut into desired shapes with a sharp knife or pastry cutter and transfer to the prepared baking sheet. Bake for 20 to 25 minutes, rotating the pan halfway through, until the crackers are lightly browned. Larger crackers will take longer to bake than smaller crackers. Cool on the pan.

Makes 24 to 36 crackers, depending on their size. Store in an airtight container, between layers of parchment, for up to 1 month. Great with any number of cheeses in this book.

DRINK ME

Cataldi Madonna "Giulia" Pecorino

Pecorino grapes, Abruzzo, Italy
Medium body, with notes of licorice and eucalyptus

There's a grape named Pecorino native to Abruzzo and La Marche, areas renowned for sheep cheese—the lore being that it's named for the sheep that snack on the grapevines. Unsurprisingly, they're a great pair. Bright, fresh, crisp tones cut through the oily, funky cheese.

Arnaldo Caprai Collepiano Sagrantino di Montefalco

Sagrantino grapes, Umbria, Italy
Full body, with notes of walnuts, porcini mushrooms, and dried sausage

Dry and tannic with loads of savory herbed-meat flavors—this well-crafted, affordable Sagrantino is a potent partner for powerful aged pecorinos.

MOZZARELLA DI
BUFALA CAMPANA
Pasteurized Water Buffalo Milk
Campania, Italy

SHAVED TRUFFLES

UPLANDS CHEESE
COMPANY PLEASANT
RIDGE RESERVE
EXTRA AGED
Raw Cow's Milk
Dodgeville, Wisconsin

FERMIN JAMÓN IBÉRICO
DE BELLOTA & PIQUILLO
PEPPER GASTRIQUE

STICHELTON
Raw Cow's Milk
Nottinghamshire, England

DULCEY CHAMPAGNE
GANACHE

FLIGHT OF FANCY

Sometimes luxury is enjoying something handmade or seasonal, or sharing an amazing experience with someone special. This flight embodies this concept. It's true that some of these items don't come cheaply, but they're meant for a splurge: a milestone birthday, romantic anniversary, or New Year celebration. Pairings hit a broad arc of flavor ripe for the lift of Champagne.

MOZZARELLA DI BUFALA CAMPANA
Notes of fresh sweet cream, with a silky, fluffy, delicate stretched curd

The moon may not be made of cheese, but perhaps clouds are made of Mozzarella di Bufala Campana. Luscious, delicate, and milky, it's a creamy, decadent canvas for the complex, heady flavors of **truffles**, dubbed "the diamond of the kitchen" by French epicure (and cheese namesake) Brillat-Savarin. The summer truffles used here are best served raw so their heady aromas and complex forest and fungal flavors aren't diminished. Depending on the season, feel free to use **white**, **black**, or **summer truffles**.

UPLANDS CHEESE COMPANY PLEASANT RIDGE RESERVE EXTRA AGED
Notes of fresh hay, green olives, and wet leather, with a rich, firm paste and washed/ natural rind

Pleasant Ridge Reserve Extra Aged is an Alpine-style seasonal treat available from fall to early winter—an "extra aged" version of Pleasant Ridge Reserve, with deep, concentrated nutty/fruity flavors that go on and on and on. It typically sees twelve to eighteen months of maturation.

FERMIN JAMÓN IBÉRICO DE BELLOTA & PIQUILLO PEPPER GASTRIQUE
You'll need jamón ibérico de bellota, honey, red wine vinegar, jarred piquillo peppers

Piquillo pepper gastrique is a much needed bridge between the compact umami richness of the Stichelton and the powerful, fat-flecked pork of Fermin *jamón ibérico de Bellota*. The sweet and sour sauce tempers the cheese and meat, which are both salty. Piquillo peppers add an earthy/vegetal undertone, which especially suits the Stichelton. A little goes a long way with this sauce, so use it sparingly.

For the gastrique:
In a small saucepan, melt **¼ cup honey** over medium-low heat until frothing and darkened. Add **½ cup red wine vinegar** and **2 minced piquillo peppers**. Simmer for 20 minutes, or until the sauce has reduced by half and thickened to a syrupy consistency. Serve at room temperature.

Makes ½ cup. Store in an airtight container in the refrigerator for up to 3 weeks. Also keen on **Ricotta Peperoncino** (see page 143) and **Monte Enebro** (see page 75).

STICHELTON
Notes of grass, toasted brioche, and prunes, with a fudgy, buttery paste and natural rind

In some ways, Stichelton is more connected to traditional Stilton, by far the most renowned English blue cheese, than contemporary versions of Stilton. Modern regulation limits Stilton to a mostly industrial affair, made of pasteurized milk in mechanized dairies. Enter Stichelton, a farmstead, organic, handmade blue in the style of Stilton, with all the complexity of flavor skilled old-world cheese making imparts. A creamy, delicate curd encapsulates gentle pockets of blue with plenty of toasty/buttery/nutty notes.

DULCEY CHAMPAGNE GANACHE
You'll need Valrhona Dulcey chocolate, heavy cream, Champagne, cinnamon stick, vanilla extract

Dulcey chocolate is a caramelized white chocolate with an über-creamy mouthfeel and notes of toasty graham cracker and tropical fruit. You won't find Dulcey in many stores—it's a relatively new product primarily sold wholesale to chefs by Valrhona Chocolate—but it's easily available online.

Ganache is a simple technique of blending cream and chocolate into pliable form. A thin ganache (made with more cream than chocolate) can be used as a glaze; a thick ganache (more chocolate than cream) makes a great base for a truffle. We're going for a thick ganache here, served in a decadent scoop alongside the Pleasant Ridge Reserve Extra Aged, which boasts scalded milk flavors similar to the Dulcey.

Chop **6 ounces Valrhona Dulcey chocolate** very fine (this will help it melt quickly) and place in a heatproof medium bowl.

In a small saucepan, cook **¼ cup heavy cream**, **1 tablespoon dry Champagne** (sparkling wine is also fine), and **1 cinnamon stick** over low heat until the edges of the mixture bubble. Remove and discard the cinnamon stick. Pour the cream over the chopped chocolate and let it sit for a minute or two. Whisk thoroughly to incorporate the chocolate into the cream. Whisk in **½ teaspoon vanilla extract** and **¼ teaspoon kosher salt**.

The ganache will be runny; refrigerate for 30 minutes or so to firm the ganache to the consistency of creamy peanut butter. Stir every 10 minutes so it chills evenly. If the ganache gets too cold and firm, let it sit at room temperature until it's workable again.

Makes 1 cup. Wouldn't throw **Gabietou** (see page 169) or **Lamb Chopper** (see page 128) out of bed.

DRINK ME
Agrapart Brut Grand Cru "7 Cru" NV
Pinot Noir and Chardonnay grapes, Champagne, France
Medium-body sparkling, with notes of limestone, lemon curd, and oyster shells

Agrapart Brut Grand Cru "7 Cru" NV is a creamy, silky bubbly with subtle floral/mineral notes. It paints a refreshing swath across the meaty, piquant, and sweet flavors of the flight. Grower Champagnes such as this one are the wine equivalent of farmstead cheese: The same people who farm the grapes make the wine. Like farmstead cheese, the connection between the raw material and the final product reflect a taste of place. In general, grower Champagnes are also a good value, as you're not paying for the name recognition of a famous Champagne house.

ZINGERMAN'S
PEPPERED BACON
FARM BREAD

RITZ CRACKER–
BACON BRICKLE

MOSTO
COTTO–GLAZED
BACON

WINNIMERE WONDERLAND

Winnimere is a pudding-y, meaty, and smoky (but not smoked) winter cheese, as hearty as a roast and just as flavorful. It'd be sacrilege to eat alone—tuck into it with friends après ski or for a cozy night of board games and mulled wine. Homey bacon accompaniments highlight Winnimere's carnivorous character, proffering sweet and salty notes and crunchy, crispy, sticky bite. Vegetarians will have to sit this one out.

JASPER HILL FARM WINNIMERE

Notes of roasted meat, campfire smoke, and forest floor, with a pudding-y paste and washed rind trussed in spruce bark

A highly seasonal American classic, Winnimere is made exclusively during winter from rich cow's milk born of a high-quality hay diet. Like most cheeses of this style, its rich, silky paste is its primary tool of seduction. A spruce bark corset keeps this custardy cream bombe contained, and adds a fresh-split firewood aroma.

RITZ CRACKER–BACON BRICKLE

You'll need bacon, Ritz crackers, sugar, unsalted butter, vanilla extract, chocolate chips

File under "Things You Should Only Eat Once a Year." Ritz Cracker Bacon Brickle is an over-the-top sweet, salty, and crunchy confection perfect for Winnimere and Boxing Day parties.

In a nonstick medium sauté pan, cook **4 chopped bacon slices** (I use **Vermont Smoke & Cure Maple Brined Thick Sliced Bacon**) over medium heat until crisp. Transfer with a slotted spoon to a paper towel to drain. Reserve the rendered fat in the pan.

Preheat the oven to 350°F. Line an 8-inch square cake pan with aluminum foil, leaving extra foil overhanging the edges. Put **25 Ritz crackers** in a single layer in the prepared pan, completely covering the bottom of the pan.

In a small saucepan, combine **½ cup sugar**, **½ cup butter**, and the reserved bacon fat and bring to a gentle boil over medium heat. Cook until the mixture turns light brown and has a nutty aroma, 4 to 5 minutes. Remove from the heat and add **½ teaspoon vanilla extract** and the bacon.

Pour the sugar mixture over the crackers and bake for 8 minutes. Remove from the oven and sprinkle **1 cup semisweet chocolate chips** over the hot brickle. Return to the oven and bake until the chocolate has completely melted, about 2 minutes. Smooth the chocolate out with a heatproof spatula and cool completely on a wire rack.

Lift the brickle from the pan by the edges of the foil. With the foil still in place, wrap the brickle tightly in plastic wrap and freeze overnight. The following day, carefully peel away the foil, wrap the brickle in plastic wrap, and freeze until ready to serve. Break the brickle into serving size pieces and serve frozen.

Makes 20 reasonable portions or 10 unreasonable portions. Store in the freezer for up to 1 month. Also sinful with **Smokey Blue** (see page 147).

MOSTO COTTO–GLAZED BACON

You'll need light brown sugar, dry mustard, cinnamon, mosto cotto (or balsamic vinegar and apple juice), bacon

What's better than bacon candy? Not much. These sticky, sweet, and salty porcine treats are basted with mosto cotto, a reduction of grape must (unfiltered grape juice—seeds, stems, skins, and all) bursting with raisiny, grapey flavor. A touch of cinnamon draws out the woody aspects of the cheese.

Preheat the oven to 400°F. Place a wire rack on a baking sheet with parchment paper.

In a small bowl, combine **¼ cup packed light brown sugar, 1 teaspoon dry mustard, ½ teaspoon ground cinnamon**, and a crack of freshly ground black pepper.

Set aside **2 tablespoons mosto cotto** (I use **Marcelli Formaggi Mostocotto**) or **1 tablespoon apple juice** and **1 tablespoon balsamic vinegar** in a small bowl.

Halve **6 bacon slices**. Dredge in the sugar mixture and place on the wire rack.

Bake for 15 minutes, then glaze with mosto cotto or apple-balsamic blend and bake for 5 minutes more. Turn the bacon, glaze again, and bake for 3 to 5 minutes more. Cool on a wire rack for a minute or two, then transfer to a folded paper bag to cool completely. Serve at room temperature.

Makes 4 servings of 3 pieces each. Also a great match with **Red Rock** (see page 179) and **Zimbro** (see page 132).

It's almost inconceivable to serve a cheese like Winnimere without bread, as it's prime for dunking, scooping, and smearing. **Zingerman's Peppered Bacon Farm Bread** minds the bacon theme, and brings a sourdough tang that's a welcome respite from the sweet pairings. Check your local bakeries for a version of bacon, ham, or prosciutto bread, as a non–mail order option.

DRINK ME
Qupé Syrah

Syrah grapes, Central Coast, California
Full body, with notes of bacon bits and grape jam

A benchmark New World Syrah bursting with sweet, intense fruit flavors. Fig, grape, and currant notes play a big role here. Spiced, smoky BBQ tones support the more savory turns of the cheese.

ROELLI RED ROCK
Pasteurized Cow's Milk
Shullsburg, Wisconsin

OLYMPIA PROVISIONS
CHORIZO RIOJA

KIND OF BLUE

These oddball blues have the umami funk typical of
blue cheese—but it's more of a meandering melody
than an aggressive hook. Standalone accompaniments
diligently back up these outliers, so that even blue
cheese skeptics will get into the groove.

WESTFIELD FARM CAPRI CLASSIC BLUE LOG
Pasteurized Goat's Milk
Hubbardston, Massachusetts

WHITE CHOCOLATE, ALMOND, & CASTELVETRANO OLIVE BARK

LIVELY RUN GOAT DAIRY CAYUGA BLUE
Raw Goat's Milk
Interlaken, New York

SAUTÉED MUSHROOMS WITH LEMON & THYME

WESTFIELD FARM CAPRI CLASSIC BLUE LOG
Notes of cream cheese, saltwater taffy, and bay leaf, with a moist, creamy paste and thin blue rind

Classic Blue Log is a compact cylinder of tangy chèvre with a texture like whipped cream cheese and a thin coat of blue-gray Roquefort mold on its rind. Salted seaweed flavors liven up an otherwise mild-mannered blue. A great-looking addition to any cheese plate.

WHITE CHOCOLATE, ALMOND, & CASTELVETRANO OLIVE BARK
You'll need Castelvetrano olives, white chocolate, slivered almonds

Askinosie White Chocolate is a single-origin white chocolate made of goat's milk powder. This bark is easy to make and a nice surprise for guests: Who would have thought white chocolate and olives were such a delicious combo?

Line a baking sheet with parchment paper. Drain, dry, and thinly slice **6 pitted Castelvetrano** olives.

In the top of a double boiler or in a heatproof bowl set over a saucepan of simmering water, melt **5 ounces white chocolate**.

Spread the melted chocolate in a ½-inch-thick layer over the prepared baking sheet. Sprinkle the sliced olives and **2 tablespoons toasted slivered almonds** over the chocolate and gently press them into the surface with a spatula. Refrigerate for an hour or so, until the chocolate sets. Serve slightly chilled or at room temperature.

Makes enough for 4 cheese plates plus extra nibbles. Store in an airtight container in the refrigerator for up to 2 days. Also a great match with **Blu di Bufala** (see page 71).

LIVELY RUN GOAT DAIRY CAYUGA BLUE
Notes of roasted mushrooms, pine nuts, and limestone, with a firm, dry paste and natural rind

There's no cheese like Cayuga Blue, with its thin streaks of blue mold in a husky, nutty paste and dank, mineral aroma of caves and caverns. Older wheels can be quite dry and almost spicy; wheels at any age transmit a musty, goaty, barnyard funk.

SAUTÉED MUSHROOMS WITH LEMON & THYME
You'll need cremini mushrooms, unsalted butter, fresh thyme, bay leaf, lemon

Sometimes a simple ingredient prepared simply is just the right pairing. Pan-roasted cremini mushrooms play into the earthy/mushroom-y notes of Cayuga Blue, while lemon and thyme perk it up with tangy, citric, sweet tones.

Clean, trim, and quarter **1 pint cremini mushrooms**. In a medium sauté pan, melt **2 tablespoons butter** over medium heat until foaming. Raise the heat to medium-high, add the mushrooms, **3 sprigs of thyme**, and **1 bay leaf** and sauté until the mushrooms release their juices, about 4 minutes. Make a well in the center of the pan and add **2 tablespoons butter**. When the butter melts, mix into the mushrooms and cook for 1 minute. Season with salt and freshly ground black pepper. Spritz with the **juice of ½ lemon**, remove from the heat, remove and discard the thyme and bay leaf, and serve.

Makes 1 cup. Also a great match with **Up In Smoke** (see page 90).

ROELLI RED ROCK
Notes of soil and toffee, with a firm, dense paste and natural rind

Roelli Red Rock is a mild, earthy cheese that's more boisterous, fudgy cheddar than assertive blue. A safety-cone orange paste smocked with subtle blue veining reveals a mild funk amid nutty caramel notes.

Olympia Provisions Chorizo Rioja brings a fiery, soulful edge to this pairing, contrasting Red Rock's soulful cheddar style with the robust, smoky, sweet flavors of paprika and oregano.

BURRATA WISHES, CAVIAR DREAMS

Burrata is like mozzarella with a smug little secret: a sumptuous center of fluffy curds and rich, luscious cream. Tangy, gamy tones turn this modified mozz into more than just a milky puff, while decadent caviar and riffs on its traditional accompaniments make this composition a stellar showpiece for winning friends and influencing people.

CAPER BERRIES

AMERICAN CAVIAR COMPANY PADDLEFISH CAVIAR & RAINBOW TROUT CAVIAR

BELGIOIOSO BURRATA
Pasteurized Cow's Milk
Wisconsin

PURPLE
POTATO CHIPS

HARD-BOILED EGG

FRIED LEEKS

LEMONY
POLENTA BLINI

BELGIOIOSO BURRATA
Notes of fresh and fermented cream, with a soft, silky, stretched curd

BelGioioso burrata is a handmade cloud of milky goodness from America's dairy heartland. I prefer domestic burrata to imported, as burrata is absolutely best enjoyed very fresh (there really isn't any other way, actually). There are too many variables to scoring the imported stuff without a risk of spoilage. BelGioioso's version is high quality and easy to find.

PURPLE POTATO CHIPS
You'll need purple potatoes, high-heat frying oil such as canola, grapeseed, or peanut oil

Fresh potato chips are so much better than store-bought. Purple potatoes add a nice pop of color to the presentation.

Cut **3 peeled medium purple (Peruvian) potatoes** (about 2 pounds' worth) into ¹⁄₈-inch-thick slices with a mandoline or very sharp knife. Soak in cold water for 30 minutes.

In a heavy-bottomed pot with high sides, heat **2 cups oil** over medium heat to 365°F.

Drain the potato slices and dry on paper towels. Fry in batches, a dozen or so chips at a time, returning the oil to 365°F after each batch. Drain on power towels and season very lightly with sea salt.

Makes 2 cups. Store in an airtight container lined with paper towel in a cool, dry place for up to 2 days. Also yummy with **Époisses** (see page 45). It wouldn't be wrong to toss a little blue cheese on these chips, bake them at 350°F for 10 minutes or so, and finish them with some chopped scallion.

LEMONY POLENTA BLINI
You'll need polenta, egg, heavy cream, unsalted butter, sugar, flour, baking soda, lemon, olive oil

Polenta blini are a cute Italian-influenced take on a traditional caviar accompaniment. These little lemony pancakes add texture, tang, and sweetness to the burrata, and are the base for the cheese and fixings.

In a medium bowl, mix **½ cup polenta** (fine- or medium-ground cornmeal) and **½ cup boiling water** with a fork and set aside.

In a small bowl, whisk together **1 egg**, **¼ cup heavy cream**, and **2 tablespoons melted butter**. Blend in **2 teaspoons sugar**, **½ teaspoon kosher salt**, and a couple of cracks of black pepper. Whisk into the polenta mixture, then add **½ cup all-purpose flour**, **½ teaspoon baking soda**, and the **zest and juice of 1 lemon**. Don't overmix.

Heat a nonstick pan over medium heat and brush with olive oil. Drop teaspoons of the blini batter onto the hot pan and cook, turning once, for 5 minutes. Keep warm in a low oven until the entire batch is ready to serve.

Makes about 20 blini. Try these with **Winnimere** (see page 174) and **Green Hill** (see page 82).

American Caviar Company Paddlefish Caviar comes from the paddlefish, a fresh water cousin of sturgeon found in the rivers of the Mississippi-Missouri River complex. The eggs vary in color from a green-gray to steel-gray and have a smooth, silky texture and earthy, briny flavor.

Large, bright orange and translucent, **American Caviar Company Rainbow Trout Caviar** has a subtle, almost smoky flavor. It's an affordable, eye-catching roe that's like the Pop Rocks of the sea.

HARD-BOILED EGG, FRIED LEEKS, & CAPER BERRIES

Separate the **hard-boiled egg** whites and yolks and pass them through a ricer. Clean, julienne, and toss **1 leek** in **flour**. Fry in the same oil as the potato chips; they'll need thirty or so seconds. **Caper berries** are easy enough to find. **Parsley** or **dill** is delicious with this presentation, but basil is nice as well. Serve in separate bowls as a garnish for the burrata, caviar, chips, and blini.

DRINK ME

Kaetsu Shuzo Kanbara "Bride of the Fox"

Junmai-Ginjo-grade sake, Niigata, Japan

Crisp, clean body, with notes of roasted nuts, sweet cream, and fresh herbs

The choice of sake for this flight is a nod to the tradition of enjoying caviar with a neutral spirit like vodka. While vodka is perhaps too harsh for such a cloud-like cheese, sake braces and refreshes the palate with a much subtler and uplifting approach. The toasty, creamy notes of "Bride of the Fox" do right by burrata.

INDEX OF CHEESES

FRESH

Cow's Milk

Bianca, Hawthorne Valley Farm..... 23

Ricotta, Salvatore Bklyn
Smoked Whole Milk.................. 146

Goat's Milk

Fresh Crottin, Vermont
Creamery 36

Fresh Goat Cheese,
Vermont Creamery 24

Up in Smoke, Rivers Edge
Chèvre 90

Sheep's Milk

Brebis Blanche, 3-Corner
Field Farm.......................... 24

PASTA FILATA

Cow's Milk

Burrata, BelGioioso 182

Water Buffalo Milk

Mozzarella di Bufala Campana..... 168

ASHED, SOFT

Goat's Milk

Sainte-Maure de Touraine 40

Selles-sur-Cher 74

Valençay 65

ASHED, SEMI-FIRM

Goat's Milk

Monte Enebro 75

BLOOMY / SOFT

Cow's Milk

Anton's Liebe Blond........................... 60

Brie, Marin French Cheese
Traditional 54

Camembert de Normandie,
Chatelain 82

Green Hill, Sweet Grass Dairy........ 82

Saint-André 40

Goat's Milk

Bijou, Vermont Creamery 36

Camembert, Haystack
Mountain Goat Dairy.................. 83

Green Peppercorn Cone,
Coach Farm....................... 142

Humboldt Fog, Cypress
Grove Chevre 75

Piper's Pyramid,
Capriole Dairy................................. 86

Sheep's Milk

Brebirousse d'Argental...................... 50

Mixed Milk (Cow, Sheep, Goat)

La Tur....................................... 106

Mixed Milk (Cow & Goat)

Kunik Nettle Meadow Farm........... 32

BLOOMY / SEMI-FIRM

Goat's Milk

Bûcheron 66

Chabichou............................... 65

Leonora 115

Water Buffalo Milk

Casatica di Bufala................................. 61

SEMI-FIRM
Cow's Milk
Tetilla............................124

Sheep's Milk
Pecorino Brigantaccio,
  Marcelli Formaggi...............163
Pecorino Rosso.....................162
Ricotta Peperoncino,
  Marcelli Formaggi...............143

WASHED / SPOON
Cow's Milk
Époisses Berthaut...................45
Rush Creek Reserve,
Uplands Cheese Company..........120
Winnimere, Jasper Hill Farm......174
Zimbro.............................132

Goat's Milk
Cabra Raiano.......................132

WASHED / SOFT
Cow's Milk
Ardrahan...........................158
Langres............................106
Le Charmoix........................78
Limburger, Chalet Cheese...........159

Sheep's Milk
Ledyard, Meadowood Farms...........87

WASHED / SEMI-FIRM
Cow's Milk
Grayson, Meadow Creek Dairy.....107
Red Hawk, Cowgirl Creamery.......158

Water Buffalo Milk
Quadrello di Bufala................70

WASHED / FIRM
Cow's Milk
Le Wavreumont......................78

FIRM
Cow's Milk
Adelegger..........................103
Caerphilly, Westcombe Dairy.........98
Comté, Marcel Petite Fort
  St. Antoine......................102
Dorset, Consider Bardwell Farm....87
Emmentaler..........................95
Gouda, Holland's Family Cheese
  Marieke Plain Young..............110
Gruyère.............................95
Gruyère, Rolf Beeler...............102
Irish Porter, Cahill's.............155
Saint-Nectaire......................41
Tête de Moine......................124

Goat's Milk
Cabra al Vino......................154
Gouda, Goat, Central Coast
  Creamery.........................128

Sheep's Milk
Lamb Chopper, Cypress Grove
  Chevre...........................128
Ossau Iraty Vieille.................50

Water Buffalo Milk
Barilotto...........................70

Mixed Milk (Cow & Sheep)
Gabietou............................32

HARD
Cow's Milk

Barely Buzzed, Beehive Cheese
Company 154

Cheddar, Bleu Mont Dairy
Bandaged 138

Cheddar, Cabot Creamery
Clothbound 138

Cheddar, Montgomery's 137

Gouda, L'Amuse "Pril" 111

Gouda, L'Amuse "Signtature" 111

Grana Padano Riserva......................150

Mimolette 150

Parmigiano Reggiano, Cravero........29

Pleasant Ridge Reserve Extra Aged,
Uplands Cheese Company 169

Sheep's Milk

Berkswell, Ram Hall Dairy 98

Bianco Sardo 151

Ewephoria Aged.................................129

Fat Bottom Girl, Bleating Heart
Cheese..125

Idiazabal...147

Manchego, La Oveja Negra
Organic..116

Pepato, Bellwether Farm 143

Pecorino Foglie di Noce...................162

Serpa...133

Mixed Milk (Cow & Sheep)

Mahon 116

BLUE / SOFT
Cow's Milk

Gorgonzola Cremificato 61

Goat's Milk

Capri Classic Blue Log,
Westfield Farm...............................178

Sheep's Milk

Roquefort, Papillon Black Label.....29

BLUE / SEMI-FIRM
Goat's Milk

Cayuga Blue, Lively Run
Goat Dairy 179

BLUE / FIRM
Cow's Milk

Grevenbroeker.......................................79

Shakerag Blue,
Sequatchie Cove Creamery..........91

Smokey Blue, Rogue Creamery.....147

Shropshire Blue....................................99

Stichelton...166

Sheep's Milk

Ewe's Blue, Old Chatham
Sheepherding Company 51

Water Buffalo Milk

Blu di Bufala..71

Mixed Milk (Cow & Goat)

Valdeon..169

BLUE / HARD
Cow's Milk

Red Rock, Roelli 179

PROCESSED
Cow's Milk

Boursin...94

SOURCES

Much of the "art" here is due to the incredible skill, craftsmanship, and creativity of cheese makers, farmers, condiment producers, charcuterie makers, picklers, designers, glassblowers, ceramicists, weavers, and countless other artisans who made the goods featured in this book. Their work is an endless source of inspiration, and it's my honor to feature some of it here. I encourage you to seek out the producers listed below, and to support the artisans in your own communities who help make the world a delicious and beautiful place.

FRESH AND FUNDAMENTAL **Bee Raw** produces single-varietal honeys harvested from family-owned apiaries, beeraw.com. **Z Crackers** produces hand-cut, all natural crackers in New York City, zcrackers.com. Baguette by **Bien Cuit Bakery**, biencuit.com. Small bowl from **Mociun**, Brooklyn, NY, mociun.com.

EAT YOUR IDOLS **Liddabit Sweets** produces handmade candies and confections in Brooklyn, New York, liddabitsweets.com. **The Botanist Gin** is distilled with for-aged botanicals in Islay, Scotland, thebotanist.com. Chambray Towelket tablecloth in White by Fog Linen, large dinner plate and small plate in White by Jeremy Ayers, layered dish by Mondays: **Mociun**, Brooklyn, NY, mociun.com. Iona cheese board from **Anthropologie**.

UDDER FROM ANOTHER MOTHER Based in Berkeley, CA, **Dang** produces Fair Trade and non-GMO certified coconut chips, dangfoods.com. **Wild Hibiscus Flower Co.** from Australia produces flower-based food products, wildhibiscus.com. Tile from **Country Floors**, countryfloors.com. Jean Marc Gady Gourmet Trio plate from **Abode**, abode-newyork.com.

LADIES WHO LUNCH (ON CHEESE) **Spoonable** produces "caramels with attitude" in Brooklyn, NY, spoonablellc.com. **Art of Tea** blends organic teas and botanicals in Los Angeles, CA, artoftea.com. Alice bowls in Coral and Violet from **Kitchen Bay**, kitchenbayny.com. Cake stands and glass bowl from **Fish's Eddy**, fishseddy.com. Teapots from **CB2** and **MUD**, mudaustralia.com.

ALL SAINTS **Fat Toad Farm**, in Brookfield, VT, produces farmstead *cajeta* (Mexican-style goat's milk caramel) in traditional copper kettles using cane sugar and milk from their herd of pastured dairy goats, fattoadfarm.com. Tile from **Country Floors**, countryfloors.com. Kam tray in Oatmeal by Eric Bonnin, ceramic hand plate by Ivy Weinglass: **Mociun**, Brooklyn, NY, mociun.com.

MISSION: EPOISSABLE Miche by **Bien Cuit Bakery**, biencuit.com. Ventana table runner from **CB2**.com. Plate by **MUD**, mudaustralia.com.

EWEPHORIC **Hot Cakes Molten Chocolate Cakery** produces organic American comfort confections in Seattle, WA, getyourhotcakes.com. Shapes rug in Grey Combo by Alyson Fox, **Mociun**, Brooklyn, NY, mociun.com. Platter by **MUD**, mudaustralia.com.

BERRIED TREASURE Wood from **PID Floors**, pidfloors.com. Plate, cake stand, bowl, Branch and Twig pie server: **Anthropologie**.

CHEESE IS FOR LOVERS **Harvest Song** imports traditional hand-crafted fruit preserves from Armenia, harvestsongventures.com. **Starwest Botanicals** is a California-based supplier of organic herbs, starwest-botanicals.com. Shapes rug in Blue Combo by Alyson Fox, fruit fork and large spoon by Lue Brass, ring dish by Zola: **Mociun**, Brooklyn, NY, mociun.com. Portrait of Darth and Girl and R2D2 Altered Plates from **A & G Merch**, Brooklyn, NY, aandgmerch.com. White rim lacquer tray in Pale Harbor, small plates, napkin rings: **West Elm**.

JOIE DE CHÈVRE **Kiss Me Organics** produces quality matcha powder, kissmeorganics.com. Baguette and Rye Ficelle by **Bien Cuit Bakery**, biencuit.com. Wood from **PID Floors**, pidfloors.com. Peacock cake stand, Red Dome dessert plate, Courtship cake stand, Temple cake stand: **Fish's Eddy**, fishseddy.com. Ruffled Rim dinner and side plates from **Anthropologie**.

BUFFALO SOLDIERS **Shurky Jurky** produces jerkys made from sustainable, grass-fed meats in Portland, OR, shurkyjerky.com. Miche by **Bien Cuit Bakery**, biencuit.com. Tablecloth from **Fish's Eddy**, fishseddy.com. Brown and white Confetti bowl by Workaday Handmade, linen kitchen cloth tea towel in Denim by Fog Linen, ceramic planters by Monty Mattison: **Mociun**, Brooklyn, NY, mociun.com.

ASHES TO ASHES **Trois Petits Cochons** produces a broad range of high-quality traditional French-style charcuterie, 3pigs.com. **The Fine Cheese Co.** is a cheese and specialty food purveyor based in Bath, England, finecheese.co.uk. Brass Diamond and Triangle paperweights and stationary tray by Futagam, Hex bottle opener by Iacoli & McAllister: **Mociun**, Brooklyn, NY, mociun.com. Jan Burtz Gold Luster dinnerware from **ABC Carpet & Home**, abchome.com. Cutipol Goa Gold White Cutlery from **Abode**, abode-newyork.com.

BELGIAN BEAUTIES **Mike's Hot Honey** is a chile pepper–infused wildflower honey harvested from apiaries in New York and New Jersey, mikeshothoney.com. Wood from **PID Floors**, pidfloors.com. Small bowls by **MUD**, mudaustralia.com. Granite plates from **CB2**. Linen kitchen cloth napkins in Denim and Navy Stripe by Fog Linen from **Mociun**, Brooklyn, NY, mociun.com. Ceramic platter from **Anthropologie**.

CAMEMBARELY **4505 Meats** is a sustainable meat company based in San Francisco, CA, 4505meats.com. **Lo Brusc** produces single-varietal honeys in Provence, available via specialty food retailer **Formaggio Kitchen**, formaggiokitchen.com. English porcelain dishes by Dana Bechert, **Mociun**, Brooklyn, NY, mociun.com. Carlo Contin Orbit Server from **The MoMA Design Store**, momastore.org.

SPRING, SPRUNG **Pacific Pickleworks** produces handcrafted pickles made exclusively from California produce in Santa Barbara, CA, pacificpickleworks.com. Wood from **PID Floors**, pidfloors.com. Natural World dessert plates, Gilded Cornet serving spoon from **Anthropologie**. Large green tray, **MUD**, mudaustralia.com.

WRAPTURE Wood from **PID Floors**, pidfloors.com. Linen tea towel in Flags by Alyson Fox, **Mociun**, Brooklyn, NY, mociun.com. Grey cake stand from **Fish's Eddy**, fishseddy.com.

PARTY LIKE IT'S 1979 Large green platter from **MUD**, mudaustralia.com.

RULE, BRITANNIA Rye & Sunflower Bread by **Bien Cuit Bakery**, biencuit.com. Homer Laughlin oval ship serving platter by **Fish's Eddy**, fishseddy.com. Blue platter and plate from **Abode**, abode-newyork.com.

THE HILLS ARE ALIVE **Anarchy in a Jar** produces handcrafted chutneys, jams, marmalades, and mustards in Brooklyn, NY, anarchyinajar.com. Alice bowl in Light Blue by **Kitchen Bay**, kitchenbayny.com. Blue side plate, round tray, and bud vase from **MUD**, mudaustralia.com.

SMOOTH MOVES Tile from **Country Floors**, countryfloors.com. Black plate from **Abode**, abode-newyork.com. Langholm cheese spreader from **Anthropologie**. Small bowl from **MUD**, mudaustralia.com.

AGING GRACEFULLY **Z Crackers** produces hand-cut, all natural crackers in New York City, zcrackers.com. Zig Zag shower curtain, Cuatro platters: **CB2**. Server tray from **West Elm**. Alice cups in Olive, Light Blue, and Coral, Alice sugar bowl in Light Blue, small bowls: **Kitchen Bay**, kitchenbayny.com.

SPANISH STYLE Rye Ficelle by **Bien Cuit Bakery**, biencuit.com. Cake stand from **Fish's Eddy**, fishseddy.com. Hirota Tokusa shot glass and whiskey glass; Hirota Edokiriko cups with lid; Hirota Karai wineglass in Red: **Kitchen Bay**, kitchenbayny.com. Cutipol Goa Gold Black Cutlery from **Abode**, abode-newyork.com.

RUSH CREEK WEEKEND Olive Petit Pain by **Bien Cuit Bakery**, biencuit.com. Green tray, Black Dip platter, Double Dip dish, Cule server, Ticking table runner: **CB2**. Sake carafes, pinch bowl: **Mociun**, Brooklyn, NY, mociun.com. Grey tagine by Roost, wooden knives, geodes: **Still House**, stillhousenyc.com.

ANATOMY 101 **Farmhouse Culture** produces fermented products using local vegetables in Santa Cruz, CA, farmhouseculture.com. Marble slab from **Mociun**, Brooklyn, NY, mociun.com. Platter by **MUD**, mudaustralia.com.

GOUDA-ESQUE **Date Lady** produces vegan date-based syrups, sugars, sauces, vinegars, and snacks in Springfield, MO, ilovedatelady.com. **Grace & I** produces a line of presses made from dried fruit and nuts in New Jersey, graceandi.com. Intermix platter and plates, cheese knife: **CB2**.

PORTUGUEEZY Tile from **Country Floors**, countryfloors.com. Tray from **MUD**, mudaustralia.com. Hirota Aya whiskey glass, Alice bowls in Light Blue and Violet: **Kitchen Bay**, kitchenbayny.com.

LOVE LETTER TO CHEDDAR **Tin Mustard** produces mustard in Brooklyn, NY, tinmustard.com. Wood from **PID Floors**, pidfloors.com. Kam Tray in Black and dinner plate in Black by Eric Bonnin; colorful dinner plate by Robert Blue; 4-inch inlaid Kaleidoscope pocket knife by Santa Fe Stoneworks: **Mociun**, Brooklyn, NY, mociun.com. Silver service on loan from Walter and Marti Spaulding.

SERGEANT PEPPERS **La Quercia** produces humanely raised, American-inspired cured meats in Norwalk, IA, laquercia.us. **Marcelli Formaggi** produces farmstead sheep cheeses, honeys, and other artisanal products in Abruzzo, Italy, marcelliformaggi.com. Tile from **Country Floors**, countryfloors.com. Plates by Colorlt Dinnerware Collection, Cutipol Moon Black Cutlery spoon: **Abode**, abode-newyork.com. Large round tray from **MUD**, mudaustralia.com.

SMOKY BANDITS **Rick's Picks** produces unique artisan pickles, including organic and kosher varieties, in New York, NY, rickspicks.com. **Olympia Provisions**, in Portland, OR, produces charcuterie inspired by traditional European recipes, olympiaprovisions.com. Black bowl from **Abode**, abode-newyork.com. Small porcelain plates by Suzanne Sullivan, **Mociun**, Brooklyn, NY, mociun.com. Black oval platter from **MUD**, mudaustralia.com.

HARD DAY'S NIGHT Marble from **Country Floors**, countryfloors.com. Blue lacquer tray, glass barware: **CB2**. Egg cup and platter by TAPA, **Abode**, abode-newyork.com.

VICE **Creminelli Fine Meats** produces Italian-inspired charcuterie in Salt Lake City, UT, creminelli.com. **Vermont Smoke & Cure** produces smoked meats in Hinesburg, VT, vtsmokeandcure.com. Streamline board with copper handle, glass side plate: **CB2**. Dark brown bowl by NO, copper spheres by Fort Standard, low turquoise bowl: **Still House**, stillhousenyc.com. Striped plate by Jeremy Ayers, **Mociun**, Brooklyn, NY, mociun.com.

STANKONIA **Brooklyn Brine** produces handcrafted, non-GMO pickles in Brooklyn, NY, brooklynbrine.com. Triangles shower curtain from **CB2**. Plates from **West Elm**.

Bubbled Geyser decanter from **Anthropologie**. Cutipol Goa Black Gold spoon from **Abode**, abode-newyork.com.

PECORINO PRESERVATION SOCIETY **Olli Salumeria** produces Italian-inspired salamis in Mechanicsville, VA, olli.com. **Marcelli Formaggi** produces farmstead sheep cheeses, honeys, and other artisanal products in Abruzzo, Italy, marcelliformaggi.com. Wood from **PID Floors**, pidfloors.com. Tile from **Country Floors**, countryfloors.com. Oval plate, napkin in Rust Flax by Samantha Verrone: **ABC Carpet & Home**, abchome.com. Mother-of-pearl cheese knife from **Anthropologie**.

FLIGHT OF FANCY **Valrhona** produces fine-quality chocolate in Tain L'Hermitage, France, valrhona-chocolate.com. **Fermin** produces traditional Ibérico pork products in Spain, ferminiberico.com. Truffles should be purchased from trusted specialty food retailers who handle them properly, try **D'Artagnan**, dartagnan.com. Bubbled Geyser decanter, Cast trunk cake stand by Dorotea Ceramics: **Anthropologie**. Divide marble server, placemats: **CB2**. Hirota serving bowls and condiment bottle from **Kitchen Bay**, kitchenbayny.com.

WINNIMERE WONDERLAND **Vermont Smoke & Cure** produces smoked meats in Hinesburg, VT, vtsmokeandcure.com. Mostocotto Praesidium is made by the Enzo Pasquali in Abruzzo, Italy, available online via **Marcelli Formaggi**, marcelliformaggi.com. **Zingerman's Community of Businesses** is a pioneering group of food-related businesses based in Ann Arbor, MI; their Peppered Bacon Farm Bread is available online via their Bakehouse, zingermans.com. Antlers candelabra, porcelain bowl: **A&G Merch**, Brooklyn, NY, aandgmerch.com. Pedestal dog stand by Eleonor Boström, egg bowl and net bowl by Workaday Handmade: **Mociun**, Brooklyn, NY, mociun.com. Spoons by Roost, **Still House**, stillhousenyc.com.

KIND OF BLUE **Askinosie Chocolate** produces socially responsible, single-origin, direct trade chocolate in Springfield, MO, askinosie.com. **Olympia Provisions**, in Portland, OR, produces charcuterie inspired by traditional European recipes, olympiaprovisions.com. Tile from **Country Floors**, countryfloors.com. Faux Shagreen tray in Celadon from **West Elm**. Hirota Karai wineglass in Violet and glass serving plates by **Kitchen Bay**, kitchenbayny.com. Cutipol Goa White Silver knife from **Abode**, abode-newyork.com.

BURRATA WISHES, CAVIAR DREAMS **American Caviar Company** is a sustainable caviar merchant based in New York City, americancaviarco.com. Striped soap dish by **Shino Takeda**, Brooklyn, NY, shinotakeda.com. Brass silverware with wooden handles, teal bowls, marbled bowl and plate all by MONDAYS, 1018 in brass: **Still House**, stillhousenyc.com. Gold tray, geobox, and placemat: **CB2**. Bull platter from **A&G Merch**, Brooklyn, NY, aandgmerch.com. Caviar set on loan from Brian and Kristen Corcoran.

ACKNOWLEDGMENTS

Thanks to my editor Jono Jarrett, photographer Noah Fecks, and Ben Knox and Christopher Spaulding of Reclaim Design, inspiring collaborators who made this book exciting and fun to produce. Thanks to designer Lynne Yeamans for a beautiful layout.

Thanks to Hristo Zisovski, Christia Goodman, Jackie Greco, and Adela Lukesova for making my work logistically possible, and to Gabriella Weiss, my best friend of twenty-seven years, for additional support.

Thanks to my agent Angela Miller of Miller Brown Griffers Literary Management, and to Anne Saxelby for sending Angela my way. I'm especially uplifted by the work and support of Liz Thorpe and Rachel Zell.

All of the breads in this book are the work of genius baker Zachary Golper of Bien Cuit Bakery. Thank you Zachary and Kate Wheatcroft for the gorgeous bread.

Thanks to Amy Thompson, Andrea Zeluck, Cristina Paradelo, Elizabeth Sayner, Eva MacLeod, Heather Davis, Kirstin Jackson, Laura Rodriguez, Lindsay Selders, Liz Andrew, Marlena Spieler, Matthew Spiegler, Rachel Frier, Rachel Snow, Richard Coraine, Safia Osman, Sascha Anderson, and Todd Cardwell for additional support.

I'll always be thankful to have known Daphne Zeppos. **The Hills Are Alive** was made in her honor.

Thanks to all the cheese and specialty food producers featured in this book, especially Pat and Astraea Morford of Rivers Edge Chèvre, Bob McCall of Cypress Grove Chevre, Bob, Andy, and Tina Marcelli of Marcelli Formaggi, Seana Doughty of Bleating Heart Cheese, Judith Schad of Capriole Dairy, Andy Hatch of Upland Farm, Vince Razionale of Jasper Hill Farm, Lynne Devereaux of Marin French Cheese, John Scaggs of Haystack Mountain Goat Dairy, Karen Preuss of Hawthorne Valley Farm, Veronica Pedraza of Meadowood Farms, Adeline Druart and Betsy Thompson of Vermont Creamery, Rachel Juhl of Essex St. Cheese, Pat Ford of Beehive Cheese, Norbert Sieghart of Kaeskuche, Glenn Hills of Columbia Cheese, Marisa Jetter of Teuwen Communications, and Goat Cheeses of France.

Saxelby Cheesemongers, Bedford Cheese, Eataly New York, Murray's Cheese, and Brooklyn Larder are central to NYC's exceptional cheese culture, and where I procured some of the cheeses used in this book.

Thanks to Adam Moskowitz, Anne Saxelby, Ari Weinzweig, Danny Meyer, Fiona Beckett, Jean-Georges Vongerichten, Jonathan Waxman, Kurt Beecher Dammeier, Marc Forgione, Marcus Glocker, Richard Betts, Talia Baioicchi, and Thalassa Skinner for lending kind words.

And finally, thanks to my son, Sterio Bax Zisovski, the most wonderful result of a good pairing.

TIA KEENAN is a New York City–based chef-fromager whose multidisciplinary food work includes cooking, writing, styling, and concept development. Her pioneering work in cheese has reinvented the modern American cheese course.

NOAH FECKS is an acclaimed food, travel, and portrait photographer and personality whose previous books for Rizzoli include *Sweet & Southern*, *Alchemy in a Glass: The Essential Guide to Handcrafted Cocktails*, *City Harvest*, and *True Thai*. He can be seen on the National Geographic Television documentary *Eat: The Story of Food* and the video series *Make Me a Sandwich*, and is the author of *The Way We Ate*.

RECLAIM DESIGN is a full-service design company providing editorial styling, art direction, and experiential and interior design. Founded by best friends Ben Knox & Christopher Spaulding, RCD creates chic and elevated environments for agencies, brands, and residential clients alike.